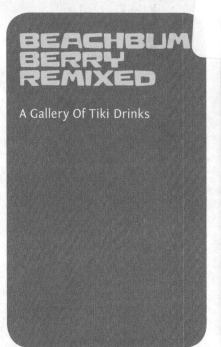

BEACHBUM BERRY REMIXED

A Gallery Of Tiki Drinks

THE ALL-NEW COMPANION VOLUME TO BEACHBUM BERRY'S GROG LOG

Beachbum Berry's GROG LOG

By Jeff Berry & Annene Kaye

Two classic recipe books in one volume, completely revised and updated, with 107 new drinks

BY JEFF BERRY

Club Tiki Press, an imprint of SLG Publishing
San Jose, California

Copyright © 2010 by Jeff Berry. All rights reserved. No part of this publication may be reproduced without the permission of Jeff Berry and SLG Publishing, except for the purposes of review.

ISBN: 978-1-59362-139-1

Design & Production by Scott Saavedra

Front cover by Bosko Hrnjak, photographed by Sven Kirsten

Original photography by Cass McClure, Jonpaul Balak, Annene Kaye, Martin Doudoroff, Kevin Kidney, Sven Kirsten, Bosko Hrnjak, Scott Lindgren, Jamie Boudreau, Greg Burman, Martin Cate, Rikki Brodrick, Brian Powers, and the Merchant Hotel.

Vintage graphics courtesy Mimi Payne's Arkiva Tropika, Ronald Licudine, Pete Moruzzi, Chip Kerr and Andy Davis, Jonpaul Balak and Marie King, Kevin Kidney and Jody Daily, Christie White, Colette Roy,

TABLE OF CONTENTS

WAITERS ORDER BLANK
(This is not a Bill)

Bruce Laserna, Sven Kirsten, Bosko Hrn-jak, Martin Cate, the Mai-Kai restaurant, Bryndon Hassman, Boris Hamilton, Mark Landon, and Tim Haak.

Published by Club Tiki Press, an imprint of SLG Publishing.
Dan Vado, Publisher
Jennifer de Guzman, Editor in Chief

SLG Publishing
P.O. Box 26427
San Jose, CA 95159

www.slgcomic.com

Printed in Hong Kong

First printing: January 2010

ACKNOWLEDGMENTS

This book wouldn't exist without the *Grog Log* and *Intoxica!*, which wouldn't exist without Annene Kaye, Otto Von Stroheim, Dan Vado, Colonel Craig Pape, Bosko Hrnjak and Truus De Groot, Sven "Sven-Tiki" Kirsten, Kevin Kidney and Jody Daily, Mike Buhen and Mike Buhen Jr., Tony Ramos, Bob Van Oosting and Leroy Schmaltz of Oceanic Arts, Stephen Remsberg, Larry and Wendy Dunn, Ted "Doctor Cocktail" Haigh, and Kevin Kearns. *Mahalo* to all — especially to Bosko and Sven, the artist and photographer (respectively) of the original *Grog Log* cover, who graciously consented to re-team a decade later for the cover of *Remixed*.

For their invaluable contribution of undocumented vintage recipes and drink lore that otherwise would have remained forever lost to time, we thank Jennifer Santiago, Bob Esmino, Julie Reese, Cathie Riddle-Weiser, Edward "Mick" Brownlee, Colette Roy, Jay Batt, and Eric Felton. For additional help with recipe research, straw hats off to Phoebe Beach and Arnold Bitner, James Teitelbaum, David Wondrich, Wayne Curtis, Hanford Lemoore and the entire Tiki Central *ohana*, Bamboo Ben, Erik Ellestad, Mark Marowitz, and the sage souses of the Chanticleer Society.

Special thanks to photo guru Cass McClure, who put such dedication and inspiration into *Remixed*'s original drink imagery. And to designer Scott Saavedra, whose talent is matched only by his patience. We are grateful to Jonpaul Balak, Martin Doudoroff, Kevin Kidney, Lisa Anne McCarron and the Merchant Hotel, Greg Burman, Jamie Boudreau, Rikki Brodrick, Brian Powers, and Martin Cate for additional drink photography; and, for vintage imagery from their collections, to Mimi Payne of Arkiva Tropika, Ronald Licudine, Pete Moruzzi, Chip Kerr and Andy Davis, Jonpaul Balak and Marie King, Christie "Tiki Kiliki" White, Bruce Laserna, Sven Kirsten, Bosko Hrnjak, Bryndon Hassman, Boris Hamilton, Mark Landon, Tim Haak, and the Mai-Kai restaurant's Dave Levy, Kern Mattei, Pia Dahquist and Hazel Quire.

For donating their original exotic recipes, we alphabetically esteem Jamie Boudreau, Rikki Brodrick, Lu Brow, Ian "Rum Ambassador" Burrell, Michael Butt, Clancy Carroll, Martin Cate, Paul Clarke, Brother Cleve, Wayne Curtis, Dale "King Cocktail" DeGroff, John Deragon, Philip Duff, Bob Esmino, Garrett Gresham, "Papa Jules" Gualdoni, Doc Haigh, Chris

Hannah, Craig Hermann, Robert Hess, Bosko Hrnjak, Francesco Lafranconi, Lynette Marrero, Jack James McGarry, Cass McClure, Jim Meehan, Brian "Elemakule" Miller, Ran Mosessco, Craig Mrusek, Sean Muldoon, Darcy O'Neil, Ladislav Piljar, Gary Regan, Stephen Remsberg, Blair Reynolds, Sonya Runkle, Audrey Saunders, Joaquin Simo, Rick Stutz, Matthew Thatcher, Stanislav Vadrna, and David Wondrich.

We also thank Andrew Hewitt and Doug Major of the Luau, Nick Camara and *Tiki Magazine*, Chris Nichols, Ann Tuennerman of Tales Of The Cocktail, Ben Gersh, Chris Patino, Tim "Swanky" Glazner of The Grogalizer, Eric Seed and Haus Alpenz, Joe Fee of Fee Brothers, Pete Wells, Steven Kurutz, Robert Simonson, Randy Wong, Arlene Eblacas of Liko Lehua, Dug Miller, Gary Hogan and Elizabeth Bell of Hawaiian Hotels & Resorts, PDT Bar, Rumfest U.K., Jack Fetterman, and the staff of *Imbibe* magazine.

This book is dedicated to the memory of Rose Epstein, the Brighton Beachcomber. *A hui hou, tutu.*

America's love affair with Polynesian Pop style was the Mauna Loa of cultural fads, a volcanic eruption that lasted forty years. This South Seas obsession began during the Depression, died with Disco, and was fueled by wildly popular faux-tropical drinks with names like Cannibal Grog and Half-Caste Kate. Don't let the kitsch factor fool you: Tiki drinks pleased the palates of food writers from *Gourmet* magazine boulevardier Lucius Beebe to *New York Times* restaurant critic Mimi Sheraton, who wrote fondly of Don The Beachcomber's "opulently intoxicating drinks." But Don The Beachcomber — and his equally accomplished rival, Trader Vic — spawned many imitators, most of whom lacked the talent and resources it took to serve a complex culinary "exotic" cocktail in all its glory. Often they didn't even have the recipes, which remained closely guarded trade secrets. So instead they cranked out inferior versions to cash in on the craze. These cheap knock-offs were the recipes that washed ashore when Tiki's tide ebbed, eventually giving "umbrella drinks" their bad name.

Because the Beachbum has no head for business, he made it his business to restore the reputation of the Tiki drink with his 1998 vintage recipe collection, *Beachbum Berry's Grog Log*, and its 2002 sequel, *Intoxica!* Since the most famous Tiki recipes had never been published, first they had to be found. Many of these were encoded to prevent theft, or scribbled as "notes to self" by bartenders writing in shorthand, so once found they had to be deciphered, deconstructed, reinterpreted, and reconstructed. Suffice it to say, the Bum had his work cut out for him. Since he is not cut out for work, this process of detecting and decoding went on for many years. So why has he once again overcome his ergophobia to update, expand, and anthologize these two books in *Beachbum Berry Remixed*?

For one thing, rum brands that we endorsed in the *Grog Log* and *Intoxica!* have since gone out of business, while new ones have taken their place. And almost to the day that the *Log* was published, cordials and syrups essential to its recipes — such as Wray & Nephew pimento liqueur

— disappeared from U.S. shelves, or were reformulated with inferior ingredients. Exciting new artisanal products have since cropped up to fill the void.

Likewise, in the last few years we've discovered alternate versions of many historical recipes in both books, some of them older, most of them better. We've also unearthed an additional 40 "lost" vintage recipes that we've been itching to share with you, along with much more — and much more accurate — historical information and drink lore. You'll find all of the above additions and corrections in these pages. We've also thrown in the five best vintage drink recipes from our 2004 Polynesian Pop cookbook, *Taboo Table*.

But that's just the first round.

In the introduction to *Intoxica!* we reported that Polynesian-themed bars were beginning to make a comeback, but that "the cocktails served in these nouveau Tiki taverns are on the whole either too sweet and watery, or too sweet and syrupy, or just plain too sweet." Seven years later, the Bum is happy to eat these words — and not just because he hasn't had a square meal in a while. Thanks to a renewed worldwide interest in classic and culinary cocktails, you can now get a perfectly mixed tropical drink in bars from San Francisco to Seattle, New York to New Orleans, and Belfast to Bratislava. Or you can just turn to Appendix II of this book, where the Bum has compiled 43 of the best contemporary exotic recipes he encountered in his recent travels to these cities, along with other new originals that he cadged especially for this book from today's most accomplished

mixologists, drink writers, and cocktail consultants.

Because the Bum has no shame, he's also included 23 new recipes of his own (he'd like to think he learned something about making drinks in the last few years, even if he learned nothing about making a living).

Beachbum Berry Remixed is the book we would have written first if we knew then what we know now. With any luck, we'll know even more in the future, and we'll have an even more thorough — and thoroughly vetted — compendium for you. Don't look for it anytime soon, though. Seven years may seem like a long time to you, but we've taken naps longer than that. Besides, we've got a reputation to live down to. So until we meet again, happy hangover!

Beachbum Berry

If you're looking for a drink whose name you already know, go to our Total Recipe Index on page 232.

If you're hankering for a particular type of drink but don't have a specific recipe in mind, proceed to our Recipes By Category Index on page 236. This index divides drinks into the following groups: rum, gin, whiskey, tequila, vodka, cognac, pisco, and okolehao drinks; hot drinks, party punches, dessert drinks, and nonalcoholic drinks; recipes for home-made syrups and liqueurs; and, finally, The Island Of Misfit Drinks (recipes with a mixed-alcohol base or other idiosyncrasies).

If you have older editions of the *Grog Log* and *Intoxica!* and want to skip directly to the new recipes unique to this edition, go to our Previously Unpublished Recipes Index on page 234. In the body of the text, we've also marked these recipes with this symbol (except for the recipes in the two appendices, which are all new):

Also throughout the text, wherever we've updated recipes with new information, we've indicated it with this "Bum Steer" symbol:

For a breakdown of the various rums called for in this book's recipes, consult the Rum Glossary on page 218.

If you see a non-rum recipe ingredient that's unfamiliar to you, or that requires further explanation, look it up in the Ingredients Glossary starting on page 222.

Finally, we've addressed any questions you might have about how to mix a tropical drink in the Tiki Bartending Basics section, which starts on the next page. (If you have a question that isn't addressed there, feel free to ask the Bum at www.beachbumberry.com)

As much as we love exotic drinks, we have to admit they're high-maintenance. Exotics ask much more of you than standard cocktails, which are a comparatively cheap date. The thing is, who would you rather spend happy hour with: Miss Havisham, or Tempest Storm?

Here's the lowdown on equipment and inventory for budding Tiki bartenders. Don't panic; the results will be worth it.

GEARING UP

You'll need a cocktail shaker with a strainer top, a heavy duty electric blender, and an electric ice-crusher. You can go green and opt for a hand-cranked crusher, but you'll regret it the first time you have to make tropical drinks for more than two people. (And don't even *think* about the old hammer-and-canvas-bag julep gaff.)

Also essential: a juice reamer. Not those scissored hand-held squeezers, which are practically useless in a Tiki bar, but a solid free-standing number with a ribbed dome and a seed trap. If you throw a lot of parties, you might want to consider an electric reamer or a lever-operated upright metal citrus press, but don't pay over fifty bucks for either option (those $200-and-up juicers are pure overkill).

The Muddler is not the name of a *Batman* villain, but a very helpful piece of bar equipment. Shaped like a miniature baseball bat, you use it to mash, or

RIVAL
ICE-O-MATIC
electric ice crushers

Model 810A

Model 800P

Model 824
Aristocrat 833

*Any season there's a reason . . . to **have an ice time.***

"muddle," fresh fruit, herbs, and spices that go in a drink. The thick wooden models are best; they're all over the Internet.

Odds are you already have a cutting board and paring knife in your kitchen, but it's a good idea to dedicate separate ones to the bar (unless you're *deliberately* trying to create a Daiquiri that tastes like garlic or raw meat, in which case you rule, and we salute you).

You'll also need a standard eight-ounce measuring cup, and a set of kitchen measuring spoons. You can find these at any supermarket, but make sure the measuring spoons go down to 1/8 teaspoon (many stop at 1/4 teaspoon). Pick up an eye-dropper at your local drug store.

Less easy to score is a small measuring glass with 1/4 ounce increments, sometimes called a "pharmacist's jigger." Vintage ones turn up regularly at antique malls and thrift shops, but the closest you might come in an actual liquor store is a shot glass pourer — a shot glass with 1/2 ounce, 1 ounce, and 1 1/2 ounce markings.

If you regularly find yourself making drinks for guests, invest in a set of metal jiggers. These are double-sided pouring cups that come in three sizes: 3/4 ounce on one side and 1 1/2 ounces (one jigger) on the other; or 1/2 ounce on one side and 3/4 ounce on the other; or 1 ounce on one side and 2 ounces on the other. We've found that using a combination of the last two (the 1/2-3/4 ounce with the 1-2 ounce) covers most of the measurement bases, and really speeds up the drink assembly process. (But don't use them in concert with the 3/4-1 1/2 ounce jigger, because it's too easily confused with the other sizes.)

No Tiki bar can do without the proper glassware: Martini-style cocktail glasses, V-shaped pilsner glasses, tall "chimney" glasses, oversized brandy snifters, single and double old-fashioned "rocks" glasses, and odd-sized specialty glasses. The Bum has never paid retail for a glass in his life, and neither should you. Hie thee hence to your local thrift shop, where you'll find all of the above for next to nothing.

Last but not least, you can't have a Tiki bar without Tiki mugs. Most mid-century Polynesian restaurants either sold logo mugs in their gift shops, or gave them away free when you ordered their signature drink, or had them pilfered by souvenir-hungry diners. In 1998, we wrote in the *Grog Log* that antique malls and swap meets were good places to find these mugs. Sadly,

nobody
loves me
but
the liquor
store....

this is no longer the case. Ten years ago
most sellers didn't even know what the
damned things were: at one mall in
Tucumcari, Arizona, the cashier wrote
"ugly face mug" on our receipt for 45
cents. Today that same mug routinely
fetches $300 on eBay, and the odds of
finding it or any vintage Tikiania in the
non-virtual world are practically nil.

The good news is, some very talented contemporary artists are now
selling new mugs online. The first to
resurrect the lost art of hand-crafted

Tiki ceramics was Bosko Hrnjak of
tikibosko.com (those are all his mugs
on the previous page; also see pages 78,
113, 115, and 121). We also direct your
attention to Cass McClure of oceaotica.
com (whose mugs can be found on pag-

es 87, 95, 153, 165, 168, and 211). Ditto the duo of Kevin Kidney and Jody Daily at miehana.com (pages 131 and 141). Google "tiki mugs" and you'll find a host of other faux-Polynesian pottery retail options.

STOCKING UP

So now you've got the hardware and the glassware, and you've already blown your budget. Allow us to make a few suggestions before you sell your blood to buy your booze.

First, thumb through this book's recipes and pick out a simple drink that interests you, one with only a few ingredients. Purchase only those ingredients; then, as you move on to other recipes, buy the new necessary ingredients as you need them. Over time, you'll amass a fully stocked bar without feeling the sting of one large, painful cash outlay.

Second, buy smaller bottles. Many spirits can be found in cheaper, half-sized 375 ml bottles; better yet, look for those tiny, 1 1/2 ounce minis. You can

avoid an enormous amount of frustra-
tion this way: Why pay $30 for a fifth
of Campari, when the drink you want
to make only calls for a teaspoon of the
stuff? This is also the best way to sample a drink you're not sure you'll like;
spending three bucks on an ingredient
you may never use more than once
hurts a lot less, and takes up less space
in your bar.

Of course, once you discover a
drink you want to put in regular rota-
tion, buying a bigger bottle becomes
more economical (per-ounce cost generally goes down as bottle size goes up).

Finally, if you know other tropaholics who need to expand their hooch
horizons, you can divide and conquer:
split the cost of a bottle, then split the
bottle.

MEASURING UP

In these pages you won't find indica-
tions like "a splash of orange juice," or
"top up with soda," or "fill with ginger
beer." The Bum has banished these
and other vagaries from his books. An
untidy idler he may be, but he is fastidi-
ous about one thing: every ingredient
in a recipe must be precisely indicated.
Why? Here's what happens when you
"top up with soda": if your glass holds
12 ounces and the drink only fills it

Trader Mort's Liquor

Visit Our
WINE LOFT

SHELTER ISLAND DR. AT SCOTT ST.
SAN DIEGO, CALIFORNIA

halfway, you'll be topping up that drink with a whopping six ounces of soda. If said glass holds six ounces, then you'll only be able to add a half-ounce or so. With so many people telling you how to run your life, do you really want your glass telling you how your drink should taste?

The other recipe direction that drives us nuts is "a dash of pineapple juice," or "three dashes grenadine." Figuring out what vintage recipe-writers meant by "dash" has become a full-time job for us (and you know how we feel about jobs). Over the last century, tropical bartenders have defined a dash as anything from one drop to a third of an ounce; when trying to figure out what amount best serves a particular drink, we often have to make many different versions of it, bracketing the "dash" amount until the drink tastes as good as it's going to get — at which point we figure we've found our answer. (We make an exception only for bitters, the one case where "a flip of the wrist" really *is* the best way to do a dash.)

While we're on the subject: since we've provided exact measurements for every ingredient, we beseech you to measure every ingredient exactly. Please don't try to pour 3/4 of an ounce or 1/8 of a teaspoon by eye, because a smidgeon too much of any one element can easily destroy an exotic drink — there are simply too many elements in play. If you find yourself without a measuring glass that has the increments you need in order to pour precisely, here's a simple conversion chart that allows you to use common kitchen utensils:

1/4 ounce = 2 teaspoons
1/2 ounce = 1 tablespoon
3/4 ounce = 1 tablespoon + 2
        teaspoons
1 ounce = 2 tablespoons
1 1/2 ounces = 3 tablespoons
2 ounces = 1/4 cup
4 ounces = 1/2 cup
8 ounces = 1 cup

Precision is also important when agitating your drinks. Shake too little and you get an unchilled, unmarried cocktail. Too much and you get a cold but watery one. Shake vigorously for at least 10 seconds, or until the outside of your metal shaker frosts. And whether you're shaking with cubed ice

We nag you with this procedural stuff for only one reason — so you can make yourself the best of all possible drinks. The last thing we want is to inhibit you with a lot of do's and don'ts, so we'll just give you one last don't: after you've familiarized yourself with the rules of exotic drink assemblage, don't be afraid to start breaking them.

Of course, to experience a drink as it was meant to be, you must stick to what's on the page. But once you've had the thrill of tasting that brilliantly crafted recipe exactly as its creator intended, there are more thrills to be had. Make substitutions. Try additions. Play. Don the Beachcomber created the Zombie by messing around with the traditional Planter's Punch; Trader Vic hit on the Mai Tai by monkeying with the Beachcomber's Q.B. Cooler. Experimentation is how new drinks are born. Who knows? Maybe 70 years from now, some future bum will be rediscovering *your* vintage recipes.

or crushed, put in plenty of it — at least enough so that it piles up higher than the liquid level.

But when using an electric blender, use *only* the amount of ice specified in the recipe. That amount is crucial to the balance of the drink; in blended tropicals, ice is as important an ingredient as the base spirit — and should be just as exactly measured. (We go through the same process of elimination to determine blender ice-content as we do with dashes; in fact, most of the unpublished recipes we've unearthed don't indicate ice amounts at all, or even whether a drink should be shaken or blended in the first place!)

Beachbum Berry's
GROG LOG

By Jeff Berry & Annene Kaye

BEACHBUM BERRY'S GROG LOG

A selection of vintage tropical drink
recipes, original creations, and new
interpretations of old classics

By Jeff Berry & Annene Kaye

INTRODUCTION

They're too sweet. They're too syrupy. They're even worse than the food. That's what your average Joe has to say about cocktails in Polynesian restaurants. But you can hardly blame Joe. The heyday of the Tiki bar was two generations ago, and the know-how to mix a good tropical drink vanished with them in the late 1970s, when the South Seas craze went south and popular taste turned from Mai Tais to Margaritas. But when an "exotic" is made properly — when it achieves that perfect balance between sweet and sour, strong and light, fruity and dry — few pleasures can match it.

What makes a tropical drink something to savor, something to revisit, something to include in this volume? First, a truly great tropical has a beginning, a middle and a end: the heady initial sip, the fuller impact on the whole of the tongue, and the satisfying finish. A great tropical also stands up to its ice content, changing flavor but remaining palatable down to its last diluted drop. And it is always pleasing to the eye and the nose. Especially the nose: The aromatic imprint of a multi-layered combination of ingredients, accented by the correct garnish, goes a long way toward making life worth living.

Hence this book. The time has come to restore the tropical drink to its former glory, especially in this era of technological burnout and cultural malaise: If we're going to feel like zombies, we may as well be drinking them.

PARADISE LOST ... AND FOUND

Mixing a good tropical drink is less a lost art than a complicated and costly one. Most bartenders simply don't have the time it takes to mix a proper exotic, and most bar owners don't want to pay for the proper ingredients. Order a Planter's Punch even in the swankiest watering hole and you're likely to get spiked Kool-Aid.

It was not always so. Master midcentury restaurateurs Don The Beachcomber, Trader Vic Bergeron, and the competition they spawned created some of the most spectacularly flavorful cocktails in American

culinary history. From the 1930s well into the '70s
— an unprecedented lifespan for a drink fad — Americans flocked to Polynesian restaurants, and not for
the food. In 1960, the menu of The Islander in Beverly
Hills offered "Pork Tiki," "Crab Puffs Rarotonga,"
"Polynesian Sacred Beef" and "Tonga Tabu Native
Drum Steak," fresh from "the ovens of the ancient
goddess of Bora Bora, Pele, Mistress of Flame." As
you've no doubt guessed by now, the big draw was the
bar. A place lived or died on the reputation of its exotic drinks, and the bartenders who knew them were
valued employees. Since their recipes were their stock
in trade, they revealed their secrets to no one.

Over the years, a mystique grew around these
alchemists who turned rum into gold. They wrote nothing down; if a competitor
wanted your bistro's bar recipes, the only way to get them was to hire away your
mixologist. But even that didn't work against the counter-espionage tactics of Don
The Beachcomber, who could have taught the CIA a thing or two. "Infinite pains
are taken," relates a 1948 *Saturday Evening Post* article, "to see to it that the ser-
vice-bar help cannot memorize Don's various occult ingredients and proportions.
Bottles are label-less; they bear numbers and letters instead. The recipes are in code
and the mixers follow a pattern of code symbols indicating premixed ingredients,
rather than actual names of fruit concentrates or rum brands. In this way, even if
a rival restaurateur makes a raid on the Beachcomber help ... the renegade cannot
take Don's recipes with him."

When Don The Beachcomber died, many of his recipes died with him. To
this day, nobody really seems to know what went into his most famous creation,
the Zombie.* But another legendary mixologist broke Tabu in his old age; partly to

• • • • • • • • • •

*Nine years after we wrote this in 1998, we finally cracked the code of the origi-
nal recipe (see page 167).

21

Exotic
Drink
Menu

help sell his own retail line of rums, drink mixes, salad dressings and condiments, Trader Vic published several cookbooks before he cashed in his taro chips.

The Trader's books reveal everything that went into *his* greatest creations — the Mai Tai, the Scorpion, and the Fog Cutter, to name but a few. And toward the end of the Polynesian Pop era, other restaurateurs squeezed a few last bucks out of the fading fad by putting out cookbooks of their own, sometimes revealing one or two of the closely guarded secrets of their mixologists.

But these books have been unavailable for decades, while most of the best recipes were never *in* print to begin with. Consequently, today's bar guides can only tell you how to make pale — and sweet and syrupy — imitations of the originals.

To fill that void, we've combed through scores of old cookbooks, magazine articles, and bar menus; picked the brains of bartenders and barflies who were there; and criss-crossed the USA to field-test the potions of the few remaining Polynesian palaces. In the course

of our research, we gained enough Dutch courage to invent some recipes of our own, and to reinterpret some vintage recipes that were almost, but not quite, worthy of reprinting. (Believe it or not, some topical drinks really *were* too sweet and syrupy!) We've included these original and revised recipes in the following pages. If the hardcore Polynesiacs among you don't recognize some of the names, that's because we followed the time-honored Tiki bar tradition of changing the moniker if we changed the recipe. For the academically inclined, the original name and place of origin can be found at the bottom of each page.

One final caveat: This collection is by no means exhaustive. Or objective. As the writer Theodore Sturgeon once said, "95 percent of everything is shit." Rather than a complete compendium of tropical drinks, these recipes are merely what we believe to be that other five percent; out of hundreds sampled, 84 drinks made the final cut.*

Of course, no two people have exactly the same taste. So feel free to alter these recipes to suit yours. But before we knock back a few, let's head back a few years.

• • • • • • • • • •

*And for this edition we've cut even more, mostly our rookie original efforts.

RUM AND TRUE RELIGION: A HISTORY OF TIKI TIPPLING

Where did the tropical drink come from? The original exotic cocktail was, fittingly enough, invented by Pacific Islanders. Order a Kava Bowl at Trader Vic's and you get a frothy concoction of rum and fruit juices. Order one on Vanuatu and you get a sticky porridge of chewed-up plant roots and human saliva. But before you send it back, consider that the roots are from the *piper methysticum*, or kava plant, a powerful narcotic that makes the world go round in that part of the world.

Although now largely confined to the Melanesian island chain, kava drinking was practiced throughout the South Seas before European contact. Elaborate social rituals attended its consumption, which was performed with a religious zeal that puts our Happy Hour to shame. The islands of Tonga, Samoa, Hawaii, and Papua New Guinea each have their own version of a kava origin myth: "The broad leaf that extinguishes chiefs" has sprouted variously from a vagina, the skin of a foot, or the hair of an armpit.

Preparation of the communal kava bowl hasn't changed much since 1773, when a naturalist on Captain Cook's second Pacific voyage observed Tahitian youths making a batch "in the most disgustful manner that can be imagined," chewing pieces of the root, spitting the macerated mass into a bowl, and mixing it with coconut milk, whereupon "they swallow this nauseous stuff as fast as possible."

This sight wasn't the only thing making British sailors sick in the 18th century. It had been the tradition since 1655 to grant all seamen a daily half-pint ration of rum, which few of them were inclined to nurse. Gulping his "kill-divil" in one manly draught, Jack Tar found himself sailing three sheets to the wind whether there was any wind or not. If the Royal Navy tried to end this tradition, they'd have caused a mutiny that made the Bounty's look like a Princess Cruise. So in 1740 they did the next best thing: Admiral Edward Vernon, nicknamed "Old Grog" because of the grogram cloak he wore, ordered the rum ration mixed with a quart of water. In 1795, over 40 years after Scottish naval surgeon James Lind proved that citrus fruit prevented scurvy, lime juice was finally added to the mix. Thus was born the world's second tropical drink: the Navy Grog, named after Old Grog himself.

In the British West Indies, plantation owners added sugar to their rum, water and lime ... creating the Planter's Punch. The original recipe has been passed down for over 200 years as a bit of Jamaican doggerel: "One of sour, two of sweet, three of strong, four of weak."

Up in North America, the Colonists were also experimenting with rum. Early drinks included the Coow-woow (rum, water, ginger) and the Bombo (rum, water, sugar cane stick), but such primitive efforts pale before another early American recipe called the Byrd: "fry six rashers of fat bacon; add one pint rum; eat the bacon and drink the syrup." The Byrd was named after Colonel William Byrd III,

Donn Beach, circa 1948

who recorded this cocktail in his journal of 1728; we doubt he drank too many of them, because he lived to see 1729.

Despite these and other decidedly non-tropical drinks (the Bellows-top Flip, very popular during the Revolution, called for sugar, cream, eggs, bitter beer and a gill of rum, beaten to a froth with a hot poker), Americans went on to make the rum cocktail their own over the next two centuries. Prominent among them was Jennings Cox, an engineer working a copper mine near the Cuban hamlet of Daiquiri — which is what he named the drink he invented there in 1896. A few short years later, American soldiers fighting the Spanish American War in Cuba hit on the notion of mixing local rum with a new American beverage called Coca-Cola; with a squeeze of lime, the mixture became the Cuba Libre, which teenagers in high school parking lots across the USA have since come to know and love and puke as "Rum and Coke."

But the greatest innovator of the rum drink was neither a copper miner nor a foot soldier. He was a bootlegger. At least, that was the rumor in 1934, when the dapper Louisiana native opened a tiny 25 seat bar near the corner of Hollywood Boulevard and McCadden Place. Nobody knew much about the real Ernest Raymond Beaumont-Gantt, and that's just the way he liked it. So much so that he had his name legally changed ... to Donn Beach, short for Don The Beachcomber.

Donn was good with names, good with drinks, and good with drink names. Word quickly spread about his "rum rhapsodies," innovative concoctions like the Vicious Virgin, the Missionary's Downfall, the Cobra's Fang, and the Shark's Tooth (forbidden love and animal dentition were both go-to themes for Donn). But it was the Zombie that really put Donn on the map. Legend has it that he whipped it up one day to help a hung-over customer get through an important business meeting. When Donn later asked how the cure worked, the customer said, "I felt like the living dead — it made a zombie out of me."*

In no time at all Donn was the toast of the Hollywood film crowd, and in 1937 he built a Polynesian palace for them to spend their money in. Don The Beachcomber's became the template for hundreds of South Seas-themed restaurants over the next 40 years, a style that urban archeologist Sven Kirsten has dubbed Polynesian Pop. "Like an island in the urban sea, the Polynesian paradise was designed to be a refuge from the metropolis that surrounded it," writes Kirsten in his *Book Of Tiki*.** "Upon entering, all the senses were assailed: Bamboo, rattan, tapa cloth and imported woods provided the basic texture. Tropical plants and palm trees with exotic birds in concealed cages served as flora and fauna, while lava rock waterfalls and their connecting streams babbled under bridges that led to rooms with strange names like Bora Bora Lounge and Cannibal Hut, where an array of found objects from all over the world dangled from the ceiling: fish traps, crates, coconuts, weapons, puffer fish and Japanese fishnet floats, most of them turned into dim lanterns, seemed to tell tales of faraway lands."

This turned out to be exactly what America wanted. Not just in 1937, but for the next 40 years. In the '30s, when most Americans couldn't afford world travel,

• • • • • • • • • •

*The back page of a 1941 Beachcomber's menu tells a different story: "The Zombie didn't just happen. It is the result of a long and expensive process of evolution ... In the experiments leading up to the Zombie, three and a half cases of assorted rums were used and found their way down the drain so that you may now enjoy this potent 'mender of broken dreams.'"
**Well, kind of. This quote is actually from an early draft of *The Book Of Tiki*, which was still two years away from finding a publisher when the *Grog Log* went to print. After eight years of petitioning American publishers who couldn't imagine an audience for his manuscript, Kirsten eventually had to go to Germany to find a patron. But he had the last laugh: Under the Taschen imprint, *The Book Of Tiki* sold out two print runs and is now universally recognized as the torch that ignited the current Tiki revival.

these exotic trappings were the closest many would ever get to the fabled mysteries of the Orient. In the '40s, when thousands of American G.I.s did go there, and wished they hadn't, the fad nevertheless grew even more popular when the South Seas were romanticized anew by James Michener's *Tales Of The South Pacific*. In the '50s, the Eisenhower era's stifling middle class conformity and paranoid Cold War culture made the lure of the Primitive even more strongly felt: In the dark, mysterious, pagan womb of the Tiki bar, Organization Man could escape the spectre of the atomic bomb and the 30-year mortgage.

Polynesiana got another shot in the arm when Hawaii was granted Statehood in 1959; by the '60s, there were more Tikis in suburban America than in the entire South Pacific. Not only were there hundreds of Tiki bars, but also Tiki apartment buildings ("Aloha Arms"), trailer parks ("Kona Kai Mobile Village"), fast food drive-ins ("Luau Chicken"), bowling alleys ("Samoa Lanes"), fashion outlets ("Boutiki"), entertainment centers ("Holo Wai Miniature Golf Course"), and even whole theme parks (such as the 12-acre "Tiki Gardens," featuring a "Polynesian adventure trail, eight fascinating shops, Trader Frank's Restaurant," and exotic creatures like "Chang the peacock.")

Donn Beach surfed this tidal wave until it crashed on the rocky shores of the emerging counterculture; somehow, sipping a Coolie Cup just didn't seem like the best way to unwind after a Vietnam War protest rally. But before the end came, Don The Beachcomber's had expanded into a nationwide chain of 16 restaurants.

32 Automatic Lanes

FABULOUS

JAVA LANES

BOWLING

3800
E. PACIFIC COAST HWY.
LONG BEACH, CALIF.

Phone
GE. 9-0958

CENTER

CLOSE COVER BEFORE STRIKING

HOLO WAI

MINIATURE GOLF
A full hour-plus-course
BRING THE WHOLE FAMILY
576 SO. GLASSELL • ORANGE

Universal Match Corp, Los Angeles

And his chief competitor had morphed from a hash-slinger in an Oakland rib joint called Hinky Dink's ... into Trader Vic, the high chief of an even bigger empire that at its height boasted over 20 restaurants around the world, from the flagship in San Francisco to such ports o' call as London, Hamburg, Bangkok, and Beirut.

Victor Bergeron freely admitted ripping off Don's idea; a 1937 visit to the Beachcomber's thriving concern convinced him to go native as well, whereupon Hinky Dink's became "Vic's Trading Post." Although Vic had never been to the islands, he assumed the identity of a salty South Seas roustabout, regaling his patrons with tales of how he had lost a leg on the high seas — then inviting them to stick their forks in his wooden one.

In reality, he had been fitted for his artificial leg after contracting tuberculosis as a child. But reality was exactly what Polynesian restaurants *weren't* selling, a fact the Trader knew all too well. He even had to go to court to defend his version of the Mai Tai, an invention other mixologists claimed for themselves. Vic won his case with this rather serendipitous tale: "I was behind my bar one day in 1944 talking with my bartender, and I told him that I was going to make the finest rum drink in the world. Just then Ham and Carrie Guild, some old friends from Tahiti, came in. Carrie tasted it, raised her glass, and said, 'Mai tai — roa ae,' which means 'Out of this world — the best!' That's the name of the drink, I said, and we named it Mai Tai."*

Although Trader Vic died in 1984, many of his restaurants are still open today. But if you don't happen to live near Atlanta, Dallas, Dusseldorf or Abu Dhabi, the best way to sample Vic's wares might very well be to mix them yourself. You'll find the best of them in our recipe log, beginning on the next page.

• • • • • • • • • •

*Donn Beach's resident Tiki carver, Mick Brownlee, told us that Donn claimed Vic hadn't invented the Mai Tai, but had stolen a drink of Donn's called the Q.B. Cooler (see page 64).

NEVER MIND YOUR LEADER... JUST TAKE ME!

AURORA BORA BOREALIS

½ ounce fresh lime juice
½ ounce Lopez coconut cream
¼ ounce orange juice
Teaspoon orgeat syrup
1 ounce dark Jamaican rum
1 ounce light Puerto Rican rum
4 ounces (½ cup) crushed ice

Put everything in a blender. Blend for at least 15 seconds. Pour unstrained into a large cocktail glass or saucer champagne glass.

ASTRO AKU AKU

1 1/2 ounces fresh lime juice
1 ounce papaya nectar
1/2 ounce apricot nectar
3/4 ounce sugar syrup
1/2 ounce falernum
1 ½ ounces gold Puerto Rican rum
1 ounce Lemon Hart 151-proof
    Demerara rum
Dash Angostura bitters
4 ounces (1/2 cup) crushed ice

Put everything in a blender. Blend for no longer than 10 seconds. Pour unstrained into a large Easter Island mug filled with ice cubes (or into a large snifter, adding ice cubes to fill).

The Polynesian restaurant craze hit its height during the Space Age. Almost every Tiki bar named at least one drink in honor of the final frontier: The Outrigger served a Flying Saucer, Kelbo's had its Star Fire, and even Trader Vic got into the act with his Space Needle. Above are our two humble additions to the Astro-Aku convergence; we based the Astro Aku Aku on the Hawaii Kai restaurant's "Sufferin' Bastard" (no relation to the original Suffering Bastard recipe on page 92), while the Aurora Bora Borealis is our version of the Fern Gully.

Astro Aku Aku | Cass McClure

THE BEACHCOMBER'S GOLD:
INDEFINITE REFERENCE

The Beachcomber's Gold is a shining example of how difficult it can be to arrive at the definitive version of a Donn Beach recipe. For years we couldn't find any of his recipes at all, but now we have the opposite problem: different Beachcomber's recipes for the same drink, gathered from different sources, all of which are certifiably authentic. Authentic, yes. But definitive? Turns out that when it comes to Don The Beachcomber's, there often is no definitive recipe: Donn kept changing his recipes over the years, and the ones he didn't change, subsequent owners of the Beachcomber's franchise changed for him. Case in point: the Beachcomber's Gold, a little cocktail that gives us a big headache.

The Beachcomber's Gold recipe we printed in the original *Grog Log* was given to us by rum collector Stephen Remsberg, who got it from a bartender at the Chicago Don The Beachcomber's back in the early 1970s. The *Grog Log* went to press in 1998; three years later, Donn Beach's widow, Phoebe Beach, and her co-author Arnold Bitner published *Hawaii Tropical Drinks & Cuisine By Don The Beachcomber*, which had a Beachcomber's Gold recipe markedly different from ours. Complicating matters further, in 2005 we got our hands on two Don The Beachcomber's recipe notebooks that belonged to guys who'd actually worked there: Dick Santiago, whose notebook dated from 1937, and Hank Riddle, whose notebook included drink prices that placed his recipes in the late 1950s. Although 20 years apart, both notebooks listed the exact same

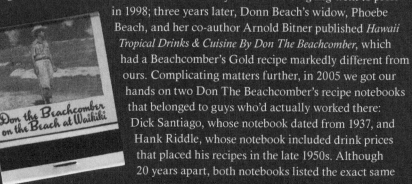

Beachcomber's Gold (Hollywood) | Cási McClure

Beachcomber's Gold recipe — which was neither Phoebe and Arnold's version nor the *Log*'s.

Three totally different drinks. With the same name. And the same author. How to account for this?

As Stephen Remsberg told the Bum, "Don The Beachcomber's was not static, and there were variations." Dick Santiago worked at the Hollywood Beachcomber's back when Donn was still running the place. Hank later worked at the Palm Springs branch, which was opened by Donn's first wife, Sunny Sund, after she'd divorced Donn and won all rights to the Don The Beachcomber's name on the mainland. Sunny would have had little incentive to change her ex-husband's wildly successful formulas, which accounts for Hank's 1950s Beachcomber's Gold remaining unchanged from Dick's 1930s recipe. But Sunny had sold the mainland Beachcomber's franchise to the Getty Corporation by the 1970s, when Stephen Remsberg obtained the Chicago Beachcomber's radically different Beachcomber's Gold recipe. Getty's bean-counters may not have had the same qualms as Sunny when it came to streamlining the Beachcomber's Gold: with its three different rums and fresh lime juice, the original would have cost much more to make than just using one rum and two vermouths basic to every bar.

And Phoebe and Arnold's recipe? After he lost his mainland restaurants, Donn moved to Waikiki and in 1948 opened a Beachcomber's there. By the time he married Phoebe, his third wife, in 1982, he would have had over three decades to tinker with his recipes — something he did compulsively, according to several of his ex-employees.

Phoebe's version of the Beachcomber's Gold could well be the end result of his experiments.

Whew. After all that, we need a drink. But not a Beachcomber's Gold. Frankly, we're not in love with any of the three recipes below. The version we like is a knock-off of the Beachcomber's Gold called the Gold Cup (see page 51). As Thucydides used to say after a few retsinas, "Definitive, deshminitive."

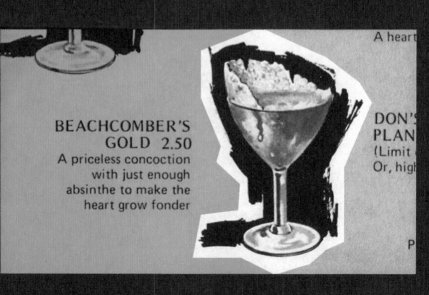

A heart

BEACHCOMBER'S
GOLD 2.50
A priceless concoction
with just enough
absinthe to make the
heart grow fonder

DON'
PLAN
(Limit
Or, hig

P

BEACHCOMBER'S GOLD (chicago)

1 ½ ounces light Puerto Rican rum
½ ounce French vermouth
½ ounce Italian vermouth
6 drops (1/8 teaspoon) Pernod
Dash Angostura bitters
2 ounces (¼ cup) crushed ice

Put everything in a blender. Blend at high speed for no more than 5 seconds. Strain through a fine-mesh wire sieve into a saucer champagne glass lined with an "ice shell" forming a hood over the glass (see next page for instructions). Serve with short straws.

As served at the Chicago Don The Beachcomber's in the early 1970s.

BEACHCOMBER'S GOLD (waikiki)

1 ounce light Puerto Rican rum
½ ounce gold Jamaican rum
1/3 ounce lime juice
¾ ounce passion fruit juice

½ ounce honey mix (see page 226)
2 dashes Angostura bitters
6 ounces (¾ cup) crushed ice

Blend and strain as above into a champagne saucer lined with an ice shell (see next page).

The final version by Don The Beachcomber, possibly dating from as late as the 1980s. (From the book Hawaii Tropical Drinks & Cuisine By Don The Beachcomber.*)*

BEACHCOMBER'S GOLD
(Hollywood and palm springs) NEW

½ ounce fresh lime juice
½ ounce sugar syrup
1 ounce gold Puerto Rican rum
¼ ounce gold Jamaican rum

¼ ounce dark Jamaican rum
6 drops Pernod
4 drops almond extract
2 ounces (¼ cup) crushed ice

Blend and strain as above into a champagne saucer lined with an ice shell (see below).

By Don The Beachcomber. This version comes from Hollywood Beachcomber's waiter Dick Santiago's 1937 recipe notebook; it's exactly the same as the recipe in Palm Springs Beachcomber's bartender Hank Riddle's 1950s notebook.

BEACHCOMBER'S GOLD ICE SHELL

Place a generous amount of finely shaved ice in the center of a chilled glass. With the back of a spoon, slowly press the ice up the sides of the glass, forming a hood that projects over the glass. Freeze glass overnight.

BEACHCOMBER'S PUNCH

½ ounce fresh lime juice
½ ounce white grapefruit juice
½ ounce apricot brandy
½ ounce simple syrup
1 ½ ounces Demerara rum
Dash Angostura bitters
6 drops (1/8 teaspoon) Pernod
6 ounces (¾ cup) crushed ice

Put everything in a blender. Blend at high speed for 5 seconds. Pour unstrained into a champagne flute, adding more crushed ice to fill. Garnish with a mint sprig.

COLONEL BEACH'S PLANTATION PUNCH

1 ounce fresh lime juice
2 ounces unsweetened pineapple juice
2 ounces ginger beer, chilled
2 ounces dark Jamaican rum
1 ounce gold Puerto Rican rum
½ ounce gold Barbados rum
½ ounce falernum
Dash Angostura bitters
6 drops (1/8 teaspoon) Pernod

Shake everything — except ginger beer — with crushed ice, then pour ginger beer into shaker and stir. Pour unstrained into a tall glass with 3 or 4 ice cubes. Garnish with pineapple chunk and sprig of mint.

Both by Don The Beachcomber. The Beachcomber's Punch debuted at Donn's original Hollywood bar in the 1930s, while Colonel Beach's Plantation Punch dates from the 1950s. The latter first appeared on the menu of "The Colonel's Plantation Beefsteak And Coffee House" that Donn opened in the International Marketplace at Waikiki.

(The Angostura-Pernod combination in both drinks was one of Donn's "secret ingredients," used in all drinks with dark rum as the base spirit.)

BOO LOO

A few small chunks fresh pineapple
2 ½ ounces unsweetened pineapple
    juice
1 ½ ounces fresh lime juice
1 ¼ ounces honey mix (see page 226)
¾ ounce dark Jamaican rum

¾ ounce Lemon Hart 151-proof
    Demerara rum
1 ½ ounces Demerara rum
1 ½ ounces gold Puerto Rican rum
1 ½ ounces club soda

Put pineapple chunks, honey, and lime and pineapple juices in a blender. Blend without ice until pineapple is liquefied. Pour this mixture unstrained into a hollowed-out pineapple filled with crushed ice (see below), or into a 36-ounce snifter filled with crushed ice. Add rums and soda. Stir vigorously until well-chilled, then serve.

BOO LOO IN A PINEAPPLE

If you plan on hollowing out a pineapple more than once in your lifetime, it's worth spending nine bucks for a Vacu-Vin pine-apple corer (available in kitchen stores and all over the Internet). Slice off the top of your pineapple, twist the corer down into the fruit, pull it out when you're a few inches from the bottom, and you're done. Reserve the cored fruit to use in the drink.

Circa 1965. This was one of the first truly memorable exotic drink recipes we found.

EASTERN SOUR

2 ½ ounces fresh orange juice
¾ ounce fresh lemon juice
¼ ounce orgeat syrup
¼ ounce sugar syrup
2 ounces Bourbon or rye

Shake well with plenty of crushed ice. Pour unstrained into a double old-fashioned glass or short-stemmed goblet (pictured). Sink spent orange and lemon shells into drink.

BOURBON SPECIAL NEW

½ ounce fresh lime juice
¼ ounce sugar syrup
¼ ounce falernum
¾ ounce ginger beer, chilled
1 ½ ounces Bourbon
Dash Angostura bitters

Shake with ice cubes. Pour unstrained into an old-fashioned glass (pictured).

WESTERN SOUR NEW

1 ounce white grapefruit juice
½ ounce fresh lime juice
½ ounce falernum
¼ ounce sugar syrup
2 ounces Bourbon

Shake with ice cubes. Pour unstrained into an old-fashioned glass.

Three exotics for Bourbon drinkers, all circa 1950s. The Bourbon Special and Western Sour were featured at Steve Crane's Kon-Tiki restaurant chain (see page 158). Trader Vic created the Eastern Sour, which provided a good template when he concocted cocktails for the opening of new restaurants in the Trader Vic's chain: The London Sour (sub Scotch for the bourbon) marked the debut of the London Vic's in 1965, and the Munich Sour (sub Cognac) commemorated the Munich Vic's in '72.

CASTAWAY

3 ounces unsweetened pineapple juice
¾ ounce coffee liqueur
1 ½ ounces gold Virgin Islands rum

Shake well with crushed ice. Pour unstrained into a pilsner or specialty glass (pictured), if necessary adding more crushed ice to fill.

OUTRIGGER

¾ ounce fresh lemon juice
¾ ounce triple sec
1 ½ ounces gold Barbados rum
sugar

Rub the rim of a chilled cocktail glass with your spent lemon shell, then coat the moistened rim with sugar. Shake the rum, lemon juice and triple sec with ice cubes. Strain into the sugar-frosted glass (pictured).

Two Tikified tipples. We based the Castaway on a 1980s rum shooter called the Jamaican Dust, late of Dorrian's Red Hand in New York; the Outrigger is a rum Sidecar.

COCONAUT

8 ounces Lopez coconut cream
2 ounces fresh lime juice
7 ounces dark Jamaican rum

Put everything in a blender and fill
blender to the top with ice cubes.
Blend until slushy. Pour into ceramic
coconut shell mugs. Serves two to
four. Ignite drink for a Coconaut Re-
entry:

COCONAUT
RE-ENTRY

For a flaming Coconaut: Remove the
pulp from your spent lime shell, then
float the shell on the drink's surface.
Place a piece of toasted white bread
in the shell, soak the bread with 151-
proof rum, and ignite from a safe dis-
tance with a long-stem match.

*As an alternative to torching
white bread, Martin Cate — former proprietor of the Forbidden Island
bar in Alameda, where he perfected the
art of Polynesian pyrotechnics — recommends dousing unseasoned croutons in
pure lemon extract, which at 160-proof
provides a much more impressive flame.*

By Beachbum Berry, 1994.

CORONADO LUAU SPECIAL

3 ounces orange juice
2 ounces fresh lemon juice
1 ounce sugar syrup
1 ounce dark Jamaican rum
1 ounce light Puerto Rican
    rum
½ ounce Grand Marnier
½ ounce brandy or Cognac
¼ ounce orgeat syrup
4 ounces (½ cup) crushed
    ice

Put everything in a blender. Blend at high speed for no more than 5 seconds. Pour unstrained into a tall glass or Tiki mug.

BUM We reformulated the 1998 *Grog Log* recipe to replace bottled sweet & sour mix (see rant on page 61) with fresh lemon juice and sugar.

By Bert Chan of the Luau Room, Hotel Del Coronado, San Diego, 1962. Chan got his start behind the stick at Trader Vic's flagship restaurant in San Francisco; this drink owes an obvious debt to Vic's Scorpion (page 85). Host to Teddy Roosevelt and location of the film Some Like It Hot, *the Del Coronado was built in 1888. It's still there, but the Luau Room is now a sports bar.*

THE DAIQUIRI: TIKI'S TEMPLATE

Rum, lime and sugar are not just the ingredients of the original Daiquiri, but the building blocks of almost every Tiki drink.

If Donn Beach didn't encounter the Daiquiri in his native New Orleans, he certainly would have done so during his early travels through the Caribbean. Wherever he found it, Donn did very well by the drink: by adding pineapple to the Daiquiri he created the Shark's Tooth (see page 86), while dosing the Daiquiri with almond and anise gave him the Beachcomber's Gold (pages 32-36). Perhaps his most impressive fantasia on the Daiquiri is the Missionary's Downfall (page 73), which heaped honey, crushed mint, fresh pineapple, and peach brandy onto the Daiquiri's rum, lime and sugar foundation.

Trader Vic first became obsessed with the drink in the 1930s. His curiosity took him all the way from Oakland to Havana, where he sat every night for a week at the La Florida bar — then famous as "the cradle of the Daiquiri" — to watch head bartender Constantine Ribailagua make the drink (see page 59 for more on Constantine). Vic went on to crank out Daiquiri variations throughout his career; over half of the 14 short hoists on his midcentury cocktail menu were Daiquiris of one kind or another.

In addition to Daiquiris from the previous incarnation of the *Grog Log*, we've here added some newly discovered vintage recipes by Don The Beachcomber (Don's Special Daiquiri) and the Mai-Kai restaurant's Mariano Licudine (Banana Daiquiri). We've also taken the liberty of updating the *Grog Log*'s Lychee Nut Daiquiri: The Trader Vic recipe we printed in the previous *Grog Log* was decades ahead of its time, but there's no need to resort to canned lychee nuts now that fresh ones are available in many supermarkets.

BANANA DAIQUIRI

½ ounce fresh lime juice
½ ounce simple syrup
1 ½ ounces gold Puerto Rican rum
Half of a ripe banana, cut into thin slices
4 ounces (½ cup) crushed ice

Put everything in a blender. Blend at high speed for at least 30 seconds, until smooth. Pour unstrained into a cocktail glass.

By Mariano Licudine of the Mai-Kai restaurant, Fort Lauderdale, Florida, 1971. (See page 136 for more on Mariano.)

Derby Daiquiri

CARIOCA HAWAIIAN COCKTAIL

½ ounce fresh lime juice
1 ounce unsweetened pineapple juice
Teaspoon sugar syrup
1 ½ ounces light Puerto Rican rum
Dash Angostura bitters

Shake. Strain into a cocktail glass.

A pineapple Daiquiri from the Carioca Rum company, San Juan, 1942.

DERBY DAIQUIRI

1 ounce fresh orange juice
½ ounce fresh lime juice
½ ounce sugar syrup
1 ½ ounces light Puerto Rican rum
A handful of crushed ice

Put everything into a blender and blend at high speed for 15 seconds. Pour unstrained into a Derby Daiquiri jockey glass (pictured opposite) or cocktail glass.

By Mariano Licudine, who entered the national spotlight after winning a 1959 rum cocktail competition with this drink (see Chapter Eight of Beachbum Berry's Sippin' Safari *for the whole story).*

DON'S SPECIAL DAIQUIRI NEW

½ ounce fresh lime juice
½ ounce honey mix (see page 226)
½ ounce passion fruit syrup
½ ounce light Puerto Rican rum
1 ounce gold Jamaican rum

Shake with ice cubes. Strain into a chilled cocktail glass.

The 1970s version of Don The Beachcomber's 1934 Mona Daiquiri, which called for 30-year-old Myers's Mona rum.

1 ½ ounces Lemon Hart 151-proof
Demerara rum

Shake with ice cubes. Strain into a
chilled cocktail glass.

By Beachbum Berry, 1994.

LYCHEE NUT DAIQUIRI NEW

1 ounce fresh lime juice
1 ounce lychee nut puree (see page 227)
½ ounce Maraschino liqueur
2 ounces light Virgin Islands rum

Shake well with plenty of ice cubes.
Strain into a chilled cocktail glass.

*Adapted by Beachbum Berry from Trader
Vic's 1960s recipe.*

JASPER'S JAMAICAN

½ ounce fresh lime juice
½ ounce pimento liqueur (see page 230)
1 ¼ ounces gold Jamaican rum
½ teaspoon simple syrup

Shake well with ice cubes. Strain into
a chilled cocktail glass. Dust with
freshly ground nutmeg.

*An allspice Daiquiri by Jasper LeFranc
of the Bay Roc Hotel, Montego Bay, Jamaica, circa 1970s. (The Bum will discuss
Jasper at length in his upcoming book,
Potions Of The Caribbean.)*

KAPU KAI

¾ ounce fresh lime juice
¾ ounce sugar syrup

RED TIDE

¾ ounce fresh lime juice
½ ounce pomegranate syrup (see
      page 230)
1 ounce gold Jamaican rum

Shake with ice cubes. Strain into a chilled cocktail glass or champagne coupe (pictured).

We were so proud of ourselves when we invented our first drink back in the early 1990s. A few years later we encountered the recipe for the Bacardi Cocktail, and finally realized that we'd "invented" a drink that had been famous since 1936. (The Bacardi Cocktail: 2 ounces white rum, ½ ounce lime juice, 1 teaspoon sugar syrup and ½ teaspoon grenadine.)

ROYAL DAIQUIRI

½ ounce fresh lime juice
½ ounce parfait amour
¼ teaspoon sugar syrup
1 ½ ounces light Puerto Rican rum
4 ounces (½ cup) crushed ice

Put everything in a blender. Blend at high speed for 5 seconds. Strain through a fine-mesh wire sieve into a chilled cocktail glass.

By Don The Beachcomber, circa 1950s.

VON TIKI

¾ ounce fresh lime juice
1 ounce gold Barbados rum
1 ounce Bärenjäger
½ teaspoon Stroh*

Shake well with ice cubes. Strain into a chilled cocktail glass.

*STROH: An aromatic, 160-proof Austrian rum-based spirit. Buy the smallest bottle you can find; a little of this stuff goes a long way.

By Beachbum Berry. After wrestling with so many vintage exotic drink recipes that called for honey, we were intrigued to find the stuff in the form of Bärenjäger liqueur. Hence this 1994 honey Daiquiri.

THE FOG CUTTER:
LONG ISLAND ICED TIKI

With its benumbing blend of rum, brandy, and gin, the Fog Cutter is the Long Island Iced Tea of exotic drinks. It doesn't cut fog so much as put you in one, which even its inventor had to admit. "Fog Cutter, hell," Trader Vic wrote of his creation. "After two of these, you won't even see the stuff."

Eventually Vic took pity on the befogged and replaced his 1940s original with the lighter Samoan Fog Cutter, diluting the original's strength by blending it with crushed ice instead of shaking.

After the Mai Tai and the Scorpion, the Fog Cutter became Vic's third most famous concoction. As such it was offered in many other restaurants, in many other permutations — not because Vic's recipe was proprietary and rivals had to guess at it (as was the case with Donn Beach's closely guarded secret potions), but because the version Vic published in his 1947 *Bartender's Guide* provided a template that invited experimentation. A Scandinavian restaurant could make the Fog Cutter its own by floating Danish aquavit instead of sherry, while bartenders who preferred lime to lemon could make the switch with impunity.

FOG CUTTER

2 ounces fresh lemon juice
1 ounce orange juice
½ ounce orgeat syrup
2 ounces light Puerto Rican rum
1 ounce brandy
½ ounce gin
½ ounce cream sherry (float)

Shake everything – except sherry – with ice cubes. Pour unstrained into a Fog Cutter mug (pictured opposite). If necessary, add more ice to fill mug. Float sherry.

The original WWII-era version by Trader Vic.

SAMOAN FOG CUTTER NEW

2 ounces fresh lemon juice
1 ounce orange juice
½ ounce orgeat syrup
½ ounce brandy
½ ounce gin
1 ½ ounces light Puerto Rican rum
½ ounce cream sherry (float)
8 ounces (1 cup) crushed ice

Put everything – except sherry – in a blender. Blend for up to 10 seconds. Pour unstrained into a Fog Cutter mug. If necessary, add more ice to fill. Float sherry.

Vic's revised version, circa 1950s. Not that you did, but if you ask us this one's much improved.

VIKING FOG CUTTER

2 ounces fresh lemon juice
1 ounce orange juice
½ ounce orgeat syrup
½ ounce brandy
½ ounce gin
1 ounce light Puerto Rican rum
½ ounce aquavit (float)

Shake everything — except aquavit — with ice cubes. Pour unstrained into a tall glass. Float aquavit.

From the Norselander restaurant, Seattle, circa 1955.

FOGG CUTTER **NEW**

2 ounces orange juice
1 ½ ounces fresh lime juice
1 ½ ounces sugar syrup
1 ounce light Puerto Rican rum
1 ounce dark Jamaican rum
1 ounce brandy
1 ounce gin
½ teaspoon almond extract
8 ounces (1 cup) crushed ice

Put it all in a blender and blend for 5 seconds. Pour unstrained into a tall glass or Bali Hai Fogg Cutter mug (pictured; Tikiphiles will recognize this as the same mold as the San Francisco Tiki Bob's signature mug).

From Bali Hai At The Beach in New Orleans (see page 111), circa 1970s. Spelled with an extra "g" either to differentiate it from Vic's original, or because whoever did the spelling was drinking one of these beasts at the time.

FOGG CUTTER 1.50
(Uncrowned king of the exotic drinks)
Carefully measured portions of choice rum form the body as dashes of lemon juice, orgeat and orange honey combine to form a purely different flavor. Sipped slowly it has no equal among Polynesian drinks.

GOLD CUP

¾ ounce fresh lime juice
¾ ounce sugar syrup
½ ounce maraschino liqueur
1 ½ ounces gold Jamaican rum
Teaspoon Pernod
3 drops almond extract

Shake well with ice cubes and strain into a saucer champagne glass. This was originally served with an ice shell forming a hood over the glass (see page 36 for instructions).

CAPTAIN'S GROG

½ ounce fresh lime juice
½ ounce grapefruit juice
½ ounce maple syrup (grade A only)
½ ounce falernum
½ ounce orange Curacao
¾ ounce dark Jamaican rum
¾ ounce light Puerto Rican rum
¾ ounce gold Puerto Rican rum
3 drops vanilla extract
3 drops almond extract
1 ounce soda water

Shake everything – except soda – with ice cubes. Then add soda to the shaker and stir. Strain into a double old-fashioned glass with ice cone (pictured; see page 74 for instructions).

Revisiting these again for the first time in 10 years, we found the original versions too sweet. Adding more rum (½ ounce to the Gold Cup, and ¼ ounce to each of the two Puerto Rican rums in the Captain's Grog) did the trick for us.

Both from the Hukilau Room of the Captain's Inn, Long Beach, CA, circa 1962. The five dining rooms of this waterfront restaurant included "exotic dishes from faraway places" in the Corinthian Room, entertainment in the Commodore's Lounge, and "quality spirits" upstairs in the Hukilau Polynesian Room.

HAWAII KAI TREASURE

2 ounces fresh lime juice
1 ounce white grapefruit juice
½ ounce light cream or half & half
½ ounce orange Curacao
½ ounce orgeat syrup
½ ounce honey mix (see page 226)
1 ½ ounces light Puerto Rican rum
8 ounces (1 cup) crushed ice

Put everything in a blender. Blend at high speed for 10 seconds. Pour unstrained into a specialty glass or Tiki bowl (pictured). Garnish with a gardenia. (The "treasure" was small pearl hidden among the gardenia petals.)

HEADHUNTER

1 ¼ ounces fresh lime juice
1 ¼ ounces papaya nectar
½ ounce peach nectar
¾ ounce honey mix (see page 226)
1 ½ ounces Demerara rum
1 ounce Lemon Hart 151-proof
    Demerara rum
¾ ounce gold Puerto Rican rum
4 ounces (½ cup) crushed ice

Put everything in a blender. Blend at high speed for 5 seconds. Pour unstrained into a tall glass full of ice cubes, or an ice-filled headhunter-style Tiki mug. Garnish with a pineapple finger speared to red and green cocktail cherries.

By Mannie "Blackie" Andal of the Hawaii Kai restaurant, New York City, circa 1960s. Once located at Broadway and 50th, the Hawaii Kai beckoned foot traffic with an outdoor waterfall just off the sidewalk. Inside, the Okole Maluna Bar featured a Diamond Head diorama with dawn-to-dusk lighting changes. Broadway columnist Earl Wilson was a big fan of the Hawaii Kai, of which he wrote: "Ask for the sentimental proprietor, 'Cryin' Joe' Kipness, who weeps at stripteasers, and he may give you the place."

HAWAIIAN ROOM

½ ounce fresh lemon juice
½ ounce unsweetened pineapple juice
½ ounce Applejack*
½ ounce triple sec
1 ounce light Puerto Rican rum

Shake well with plenty of ice cubes. Strain into a chilled cocktail glass.

*APPLEJACK: An apple brandy marketed by Laird's.

From the Hawaiian Room of the Hotel Lexington, New York City, circa 1940s. Swiss chefs created the Hawaiian Room's "authentic Polynesian food," but the dancers were imported from Tahiti. The floor show was an instant success upon its 1937 debut, launching the career of Hilo Hattie and later featuring Steve Allen, who broadcast a live TV show from the Hawaiian Room stage in the mid-1950s.

HELL IN THE PACIFIC

¾ ounce fresh lime juice
½ ounce maraschino liqueur
¼ ounce pomegranate syrup (see page 230)
1 ½ ounces Lemon Hart 151-proof Demerara rum

Shake well with plenty of crushed ice. Pour unstrained into a pilsner glass. Garnish with American and Japanese flags stuck to a lime wedge (pictured opposite).

NOA NOA

1 ounce fresh lime juice
½ ounce demerara sugar syrup (see page 225)
4 to 6 mint leaves
3 ounces Demerara rum

Swizzle everything in a double old-fashioned glass partly filled with crushed ice. Add more crushed ice to fill. Swizzle again until glass frosts. Garnish with a mint sprig and your spent lime shell.

PLANET OF THE APES

½ ounce fresh lime juice
1 ounce unsweetened pineapple juice
1 ounce orange juice
¾ ounce crème de banana
1 ounce dark Jamaican rum
½ ounce amber 151-proof rum (such as Cruzan, El Dorado, or Bacardi)

Shake well with plenty of ice. Pour unstrained into a tall glass. Garnish with a slice of fresh banana speared to a cocktail cherry. Top with a purple orchid.

In the tradition of early Tiki bartists who took Caribbean recipes and adapted them into faux-Polynesian punches, here's our take on three West Indian classics. We tweaked the Myrtle Bank Punch, a 1920s specialty of the Myrtle Bank Hotel in Jamaica, into the Hell In The Pacific. We based the Noa Noa on another 1920s drink, the Queen's Park Swizzle of the Queen's Park Hotel, Trinidad; the Planet Of The Apes evolved from a midcentury Caribbean cooler called the West Indian Punch.

HURRICANE

2 ounces fresh lemon juice
2 ounces passion fruit syrup
4 ounces dark Jamaican rum

Shake well with plenty of crushed ice.
Pour unstrained into a hurricane glass
(pictured opposite) or large Tiki mug,
adding more ice to fill.

RUM RUNNER

1 ½ ounces fresh lime juice
7/8 ounce blackberry brandy
7/8 ounce crème de banana
5/8 ounce grenadine
¾ ounce 151-proof Caribbean
    rum (Cruzan or Bacardi)

Fill your blender halfway with ice
cubes. Add above ingredients.
Blend until smooth. Pour into a pint
glass or Tiki mug (pictured).

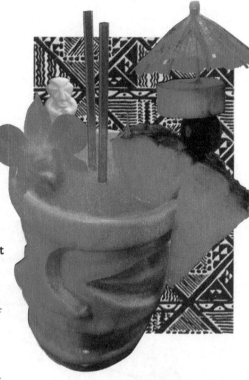

*Two legendary tropicals born south of
the Mason-Dixon Line.*

*The Hurricane hails from Pat
O'Brien's restaurant in New Orleans,
circa 1940s. Whiskey was in short supply after WWII, while liquor distributors
were awash in rum; their solution was to force bars to buy a case of rum with every
Scotch purchase. The story goes that Pat O'Brien's head bartender, Louis Culligan,
came up with the Hurricane as a way to get rid of all that unwanted rum. Pat's is still
a thriving concern in the French Quarter, but these days its Hurricane is made from a
noxious cherry-flavored bottled mix. Go for the lovely patio garden, but order a beer.*

*In 1972, "Tiki John" Ebert created the Rum Runner at the Holiday Isle Resort in
the Florida Keys. Back then customers mixed their own drinks from bottles left out on
the Holiday Isle bar; Ebert cobbled together the leftover ingredients — improvising a
drink so popular it now has its own T-shirt at the Holiday Isle gift shop.*

Hurricane

KRAKATOA

1 ½ ounces fresh lime juice
1 ounce orange juice
1 ounce grapefruit juice
1 ounce apricot nectar
½ ounce falernum
Teaspoon coffee liqueur

1 ½ ounces gold Puerto Rican rum
1 ½ ounces Demerara rum
Dash Angostura bitters
2 ounces Kona coffee, chilled
1 cup (8 ounces) crushed ice

Put everything — except Kona coffee — in a blender. Blend for up to 10 seconds. Pour unstrained into a 36-ounce snifter filled with ice cubes. Float coffee.

One of our favorite exotics is the Mutiny, a tangy long drink laced with coffee; it's a specialty of the Mai-Kai in Fort Lauderdale, from whom we couldn't pry the recipe at any price when we first encountered the drink in 1993. (It didn't help negotiations that we were broke at the time.) But two years later we discovered that if we took a midcentury recipe for the Hawaii Kai Swizzle, late of the Hawaii Kai in New York (see page 52), subbed coffee liqueur for the Swizzle's sugar syrup, and added a float of iced Joe, the result — while not likely to incite a Mutiny — was not in the least unpleasant.

TORTUGA

½ ounce orange juice
½ ounce fresh lime juice
½ ounce fresh lemon juice
½ ounce orange Curacao
½ ounce white crème de cacao
¼ ounce grenadine
1 ounce Italian vermouth
1 ounce Lemon Hart 151-proof Demerara rum
1 ounce 123-proof Cuban rum (sub ¾ ounce 151-proof Bacardi rum)

LA FLORIDA COCKTAIL

1 ounce fresh lime juice
½ ounce Italian vermouth
¼ ounce white crème de cacao
Teaspoon orange Curacao
Teaspoon grenadine
1 ounce light Puerto Rican rum

Shake everything with ice cubes. Strain into a pilsner glass filled with crushed ice (pictured). Garnish with a lime wedge.

Shake well with ice cubes. Strain into a saucer champagne glass. Garnish with a twist of orange peel.

Not until until we started putting this revised edition together did we notice how Trader Vic used the La Florida Cocktail's unique vermouth-cacao-Curacao-grenadine combination as the foundation for the Tortuga:

The La Florida Cocktail was created by Constantine Ribailagua of La Florida bar in Havana (pictured above), circa 1930s, when Constantine numbered Ernest Hemingway and Trader Vic among his fans. Known as "El Rey de los Coteleros," or "The Cocktail King," Constantine reportedly squeezed 80 million limes and poured 10 million Daiquiris during his 40-year tenure at La Florida, which ended with his death in 1952. Trader Vic must have sampled the La Florida Cocktail when he visited Havana in the 1930s, because he later put the drink on his cocktail menu; later still, he put the La Florida's unique flavor profile to work in the Tortuga (circa 1948).

LANI-HONI

½ ounce fresh lemon juice
1 ounce light Puerto Rican rum
1 ½ ounces Bénédictine

Shake with ice cubes. Strain into a small wine goblet filled with fresh crushed ice.

MARIPOSA FIZZ
NEW

½ ounce fresh lemon juice
¼ ounce sugar syrup
¼ ounce white crème de cacao
1 ½ ounces gin
1 egg white (see page 225)
orange flower water
soda water

Rinse a tall glass with orange flower water and set glass aside. In a cocktail shaker half-filled with ice cubes, shake gin, lemon juice, sugar syrup, crème de cacao and egg white. Strain into glass. Add 1 ½ ounces soda water (or more to taste), fill glass with ice, and dust with freshly grated nutmeg.

Both as served aboard the Matson Line's SS Mariposa on its 42-day South Seas cruise, circa 1962. Four Matson cruise ships once "plied the blue Pacific" in "yacht-like voyages to ports of paradise," sailing from San Francisco to Bora Bora, Tahiti, Rarotonga, Fiji, Pago Pago, New Caledonia and New Zealand.

THE LAPU LAPU: HAIL TO THE CHIEF

Who does a guy have to kill to get a drink named after him? In the case of Chief Lapu Lapu, it was a simple matter of wasting Ferdinand Magellan when the great Portuguese navigator dropped anchor in the Philippines in 1521.

Apparently Magellan had it coming. Not content with being the first European to discover the Philippines, he tried to strong-arm the locals into surrendering to Spain (under whose flag he sailed) and converting to Christianity. Lapu Lapu, a Muslim, would have none of it; armed only with knives, his men defeated Magellan's despite their cannon and blunderbusses. No European set foot on Philippine soil for the next 54 years, and Lapu Lapu became the first national hero of the islands.

We don't know who invented the drink, or where it originated. It first appeared on Polynesian restaurant menus in the 1950s, and was almost always served as a communal drink for two or more. The Chief went through several personality changes over the decades; here are the three best sides of him that we've encountered.

CHIEF LAPU LAPU

3 ounces orange juice	1 ounce passion fruit syrup
2 ounces fresh lemon juice	1 ½ ounces dark Jamaican rum
1 ounce sugar syrup	1 ½ ounces light Puerto Rican rum

Shake well with ice cubes and pour into a large snifter. Add more ice to fill (pictured next page).

The standard midcentury version.

Instead of the fresh lemon juice and sugar syrup listed above, the 1998 Grog Log *recipe called for 3 ounces of bottled sweet & sour. We've gone from tolerating the chemical taste of commercial sweet & sour (for convenience's sake) to banishing it from our bar (for the sake of all that is holy). We implore you to do the same.*

Chief Lapu Lapu

AKU AKU LAPU

1 ounce fresh lemon juice
1 ounce unsweetened pineapple juice
1 ounce white grapefruit juice
1 ounce orange juice
1 ounce falernum
1 ounce gold Puerto Rican rum
1 ounce dark Jamaican rum
1 ounce Lemon Hart 151-proof
    Demerara rum
16 ounces (2 cups) crushed ice

Put everything in a blender. Blend at high speed for about 20 seconds. Pour into a large snifter or Tiki bowl, adding ice cubes to fill. Garnish with a gardenia. Serves two.

A more elaborate interpretation from from the Aku Aku restaurant, Las Vegas, circa 1960.

KIKUYA LAPU

¼ ounce cranberry juice
½ ounce fresh lime juice
¾ ounce orange juice
¾ ounce unsweetened pineapple juice
¾ ounce grapefruit juice
¾ ounce passion fruit syrup
¾ ounce honey mix (see page 226)
1 ½ ounces dark Jamaican rum
½ ounce 151-proof Caribbean rum
    (Cruzan or Bacardi)
Dash Angostura bitters
6 drops (1/8 teaspoon) Pernod
3 drops almond extract

Shake everything with plenty of ice. Pour unstrained into a snifter or Tiki bowl, adding more ice to fill. Garnish with pineapple, cherry, mint, and a paper parasol.

Created in 1992 by Bob Esmino (pictured) for the Kikuya restaurant, Huntington Beach, California. From 1958 to 1964, Bob was a bar manager for Steve Crane's Kon-Tiki Ports restaurant chain, spending two years each in the Portland, Cleveland, and Chicago Kon-Tikis. We owe him a huge debt of gratitude, because he provided most of the "lost" Kon-Tiki recipes in this book and in Sippin' Safari (which devotes an entire chapter to Bob's life and career).

Join
me in a...

MAI TAI

...the flavor of tropical fruits,
spices and tangy-sweet limes...
blended with the finest rum
to make a relaxing, refreshing
Island cocktail.

Original

DON THE
BEACHCOMBER

THE MAI TAI: WHO'S YOUR DADDY?

The Mai Tai war has raged for over half a century, and it ain't over yet. New books
and magazine articles continue to fan the flames of conflict between the combat-
ants, even though most of them are dead and buried.

Bandleader Harry Owens claimed he introduced the Mai Tai to the world in
1954. Trader Vic claimed he invented the Mai Tai in 1944, and in 1970 won a court
case to prove it. That verdict aside, Donn Beach's widow Phoebe Beach insists that
Donn invented the Mai Tai in 1933.

At the risk of getting fragged in the crossfire, let's examine the evidence.

Harry Owens, in his memoir *Sweet Leilani*, tells how in 1954 he and his friend
Andy Geer, with assistance from James Michener and a Royal Hawaiian Hotel

bartender named Kawika, attempted to re-create a drink that Geer had encountered in Tahiti. The drink was called the Mai Tai. The boys eventually hit on a formula of three rums, Curacao, falernum, orgeat and sugar. "In the years to come," wrote Owens, "the world learned to love this Geer-Owens re-creation." Aside from the lack of lime juice, this story suffers from a lack of credibility. Why? Because Trader Vic had brought *his* Mai Tai to the Royal Hawaiian one year earlier, at the behest of the Matson cruise ship company (see page 60), which then owned the Royal Hawaiian. In 1954, all Owens would have had to do to "re-create" a Mai Tai was order one off the cocktail menu.

According to Trader Vic, the Mai Tai was born 10 years earlier in his Oakland bar. In his autobiography, Vic recounts how one night in 1944 he and his bartender decided to create "the finest drink we could make." Before the night was over, they'd done just that. Vic served the result to two friends from Tahiti, who pronounced it "*mai tai*," Tahitian for "the best." Frankly, we've read accounts of Bigfoot sightings that sound more convincing. But there's no denying that Vic — one way or another — did come up with a lovely drink. So much so that Mai Tais soon appeared in bars the world over. Since these bars didn't have Vic's top-secret recipe, they were only partially fibbing when they claimed authorship: Umpteen different midcentury Mai Tai formulas were improvised to satisfy customer demand for Vic's "in" drink, resulting in Mai Tais that were Mai Tais in name only. "This aggravates my ulcer completely," Vic wrote in the updated 1972 version of his *Bartender's Guide*, in which he finally revealed his recipe. "Anybody who

meet exotic
MAI TAI
the NEW bottled cocktail

READY-TO-SERVE!...

LEMON
HART

MAI TAI
COCKTAIL

This island mystery combines the flavor of exotic tropical fruits with the unique character of Jamaica Rum —all blended with the care and secrecy of a Polynesian tribal potion.

Just fill a large old-fashioned glass with ice—Pour in Lemon Hart's new ready-to-serve Mai Tai Cocktail and have your own Luau tonight.

LEMON HART
MAI TAI
COCKTAIL

says I didn't create this drink is a dirty stinker."

Vic had put his money where his mouth was two years earlier, when he filed a lawsuit against the Sun-Vac Corporation. Sun-Vac had licensed the Don The Beachcomber name to put on the label of their bottled tropical drink pre-mixes, one of which was for a Mai Tai. Vic challenged their claim that the drink originated at Don The Beachcomber's, and eventually won an out-of-court settlement.

In her 2002 book, *Hawaii Tropical Rum Drinks & Cuisine By Don The Beachcomber*, Phoebe Beach disputes Vic's claim, court case or no court case. She and co-author Arnold Bitner offer two key pieces of evidence.

The first is a 1989 letter that newspaperman Jim Bishop sent to the *Honolulu Advertiser*, in which Bishop recalled: "In probably 1970 or 1971 Donn and I were with Vic at Vic's in San Francisco ... Vic said in effect that night, 'Blankety blank, Donn, I wished you'd never come up with the blankety blank thing. It's caused me a lot of arguing with people.'" That "thing" was the Mai Tai. Now, far be it from us to question an eyewitness account from a fellow member of the Fourth Estate. But why would Vic, in the same year he fought a legal battle to prove he created the Mai Tai, reverse himself in the presence of a nationally syndicated columnist like Bishop? Especially when Vic had just trumpeted his authorship of the Mai Tai to another columnist, Eddie Sherman of the *Honolulu Star-Bulletin*? Again, no offense to Mr. Bishop. Just throwin' it out there.

And no disrespect to Phoebe Beach and Arnold Bitner — whose book contains priceless information

"I'm much easier to make than I used to be."

"For a long time people wouldn't even try. They thought I was too...difficult. But Trader Vic knows my secret (he should—he invented me!) He's put just the right blend of three prize rums in one bottle, just the right combination of tropical fruit (double-strength, goes twice as far!) in another. Want to try me?"

Pour equal portions of Trader Vic's Mai Tai Rum and Trader Vic's Mai Tai Mix into a glass crammed with ice. Then sit back and relax. You've got it made.

TRADER VIC'S® Free Recipe Booklet: 2834 Eighth St. Berkeley, Calif.

Jules Berman & Assoc., Beverly Hills, Calif.

Mai Tai Rum 86 Proof.

about Donn, and rescues many lost recipes to boot — but their second piece of evidence also vexes us. This is a Mai Tai recipe by Donn himself, purportedly invented in 1933. However, there is no Mai Tai listed on any Don The Beachcomber's menu printed before the Kennedy era. At least, not any Beachcomber's menu *we've* seen, and we've seen quite a few. When we contacted Phoebe and Arnold about this, they referred us to an article in the October 2006 issue of *Aloha Spirit* magazine, which reprints what the magazine claims is a 1941 Beachcomber's menu offering a Mai Tai. But the menu is closer to 1961 than 1941. On this menu a Beachcomber's Punch costs $1.10, while a 1940 menu in the Bum's collection lists the same drink for 60 cents. (The *Aloha Spirit* menu's 1941 copyright date is irrelevant, since every Beachcomber's menu printed between that year and the late 1970s carries a 1941 copyright.)

Besides the Mai Tai, there are two other items on this menu that raise a red flag: a Scorpion and a Fog Cutter. No one disputes that these two drinks were in-

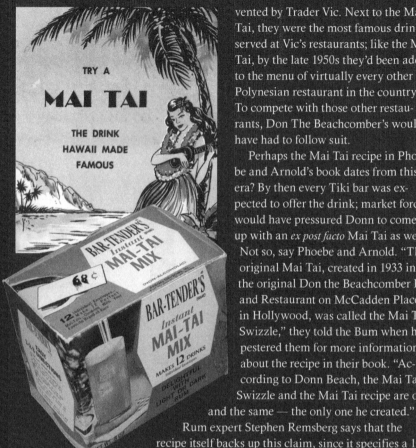

TRY A

MAI TAI

THE DRINK
HAWAII MADE
FAMOUS

vented by Trader Vic. Next to the Mai Tai, they were the most famous drinks served at Vic's restaurants; like the Mai Tai, by the late 1950s they'd been added to the menu of virtually every other Polynesian restaurant in the country. To compete with those other restaurants, Don The Beachcomber's would have had to follow suit.

Perhaps the Mai Tai recipe in Phoebe and Arnold's book dates from this era? By then every Tiki bar was expected to offer the drink; market forces would have pressured Donn to come up with an *ex post facto* Mai Tai as well. Not so, say Phoebe and Arnold. "The original Mai Tai, created in 1933 in the original Don the Beachcomber Bar and Restaurant on McCadden Place in Hollywood, was called the Mai Tai Swizzle," they told the Bum when he pestered them for more information about the recipe in their book. "According to Donn Beach, the Mai Tai Swizzle and the Mai Tai recipe are one and the same — the only one he created."

Rum expert Stephen Remsberg says that the recipe itself backs up this claim, since it specifies a 10-year-aged premium rum called Myers's Plantation. "Myers's Plantation appeared in a couple of old Jamaican duty-free price lists in the '30s," notes Stephen. "I've seen no reference to it later than 1939."

Phoebe added one interesting detail about the Donn Beach Mai Tai: "It was not one of his favorites." If this was the case, could he have cut the Mai Tai from his repertoire early on? This would account for its absence from the surviving Beachcomber's menus. But if the Mai Tai *wasn't* on the menu, then how would Vic have been exposed to it in the first place? He couldn't steal it if it wasn't there to steal.

Further evidence suggests that Vic never had the opportunity to sample Donn's Mai Tai. Vic originally got the idea to open a Polynesian restaurant after a visit to Don The Beachcomber's in 1937; as luck would have it, the Bum possesses a 1937 Don The Beachcomber's recipe notebook, which waiter Dick Santiago carried in his shirt pocket during his tenure at the Beachcomber's. There is no Mai Tai or Mai Tai Swizzle among the notebook's 70 recipes. Even more to the point, Vic's Mai Tai doesn't taste much like Donn's.

So where does this leave us? With a sitcom coincidence worthy of *Gilligan's Island:* Donn Beach, who had spent time in Tahiti, creates a drink which he names after a common Tahitian adjective — the same adjective spoken by a Tahitian couple to describe a drink created by Trader Vic, who then gives *his* drink that name. Cue laugh track as hilarious complications ensue: Donn says he invented the Mai Tai. This is true. Vic says he invented the Mai Tai. This is also true.

But the whole truth is that while Donn created *a* Mai Tai, Vic created *the* Mai Tai — independently of Donn.

Or did he? Another front in the Mai Tai war opened up when, while researching our book *Sippin' Safari*, we crossed paths with Edward "Mick" Brownlee. Mick, who worked closely with Donn for over 10 years, told us that Donn never said Vic stole the Mai Tai from him. What Donn *did* say was that Vic stole a drink of Donn's called the Q.B. Cooler, which Vic then *named* the Mai Tai. This prompted us to revisit our 1937 Beachcomber's recipe notebook. Sure enough, there was the Q.B. Cooler ... written down in longhand, during the very same year that Vic would have encountered it on his 1937 visit to the Beachcomber's. We whipped up a Q.B., and damned if it didn't taste like a Trader Vic's Mai Tai — much more so than the Donn Beach Mai Tai Swizzle.

After Vic's Mai Tai became such a big money-maker, the irony that Donn had actually created its famous flavor — in the form of the Q.B. Cooler — must have galled Donn no end. (Ever the gentleman, Donn refused to discuss the issue in public. Whenever Trader Vic's name came up, he always said, "I am pleased to ignore him.")

So who wins the Mai Tai war? While Vic may have set out to clone Donn's Q.B. Cooler, the only ingredients the Q.B. and Vic's Mai Tai have in common are lime juice and rum — and not even the same rum. It took considerable skill on Vic's part to create a wholly independent formula from the Q.B. that still tasted as good, if not better, than the Q.B. (You can judge for yourself by making the Q.B. recipe on page 84.) By this yardstick, the victor is Victor.

But not so fast. We're forgetting one very important thing here. Phoebe Beach was married to Donn, while we never even met the guy. If Donn's wife says Donn told her he invented a drink called the Mai Tai in 1933, and that this is the drink Vic appropriated, then who are we to argue? That would be the height of arrogance, and arrogance is one attitude a bum can ill afford to cop.

So make what you will of the above assertions, objections, conjectures. As for us, we'll make a Mai Tai. Trader Vic's, if you please: whether or not it's the first of the recipes listed below, it's by far the best.

Mai Tai from The Waikiki Outrigger Hotel

Trader Vic Mai Tai

MAI TAI (Trader Vic)

1 ounce fresh lime juice
½ ounce orange Curacao
¼ ounce orgeat syrup
¼ ounce sugar syrup
1 ounce dark Jamaican rum
1 ounce amber Martinique rum

Shake well with plenty of crushed ice. Pour unstrained into a double old-fashioned glass. Sink your spent lime shell into drink. Garnish with a mint sprig. (Pictured opposite.)

Invented by Trader Vic at his Oakland bar (pictured above), 1944.

MAI TAI SWIZZLE (Don The Beachcomber) NEW

1 ounce grapefruit juice
¾ ounce fresh lime juice
½ ounce Cointreau
¼ ounce falernum
1 ½ ounces Myers's Plantation rum

(sub Myers's Legend 10-year)
1 ounce Cuban rum (sub gold Virgin Islands)
6 drops (1/8 teaspoon) Pernod
Dash Angostura bitters

Shake well with crushed ice. Pour unstrained into a double old-fashioned glass. Garnish with 4 mint sprigs.

By Don The Beachcomber, circa 1933, from Phoebe Beach and Arnold Bitner's book Hawaii Tropical Rum Drinks & Cuisine By Don The Beachcomber.

MAI TAI
(Royal Hawaiian)

1 ounce orange juice
1 ounce unsweetened pineapple juice
½ ounce fresh lime juice
¼ ounce fresh lemon juice
¼ ounce orange Curacao
¼ ounce orgeat syrup
¼ ounce sugar syrup
1 ounce Demerara rum
1 ounce dark Jamaican rum
1 ounce light Puerto Rican rum

Shake with plenty of crushed ice. Pour unstrained into a double old-fashioned glass. Garnish with a pineapple finger, sugar cane stick, orchid, and mint sprig.

From the Surf Bar of the Royal Hawaiian Hotel, where Trader Vic introduced his Mai Tai to the islands in 1953. Over the ensuing years, this recipe (which dates from 1971) no doubt evolved from Vic's into its present form.

MAI TAI (stuft shirt) NEW

¼ ounce fresh lemon juice
¼ ounce unsweetened pineapple juice
¼ ounce orange juice
¼ ounce grenadine
½ ounce Sauternes*

½ ounce dark Jamaican rum
1 ounce gold Barbados rum
3 teaspoons amber 151-proof rum
    (Cruzan, El Dorado, or Bacardi)

Shake with ice cubes. Pour unstrained into an old-fashioned glass. Garnish with a mint sprig and pineapple spear.

*SAUTERNES: A pricey French dessert wine. You can substitute Monbazillac, which wine-sellers often refer to as "poor man's Sauternes."

Stuft Shirt
RESTAURANT

From the Stuft Shirt restaurants, Pasadena and Newport Beach, California, circa 1960s. We didn't plan on including examples of the many mangled Mai Tais that popped up in Vic's wake, but we couldn't resist this one. The Stuft Shirt's off-the-rails recipe commits every sin in the bogus Mai Tai playbook — pineapple juice, orange juice, grenadine — and then adds insult to injury with Sauternes. The joke is, the result isn't bad. Certainly not a Mai Tai, but if you called it something else it would be a decent pre-prandial tipple.

MISSIONARY'S DOWNFALL

½ ounce fresh lime juice
½ ounce peach brandy
1 ounce honey mix (see page 226)
1 ounce light Puerto Rican rum

2 ounces (¼ cup) diced fresh pineapple
2 ounces (¼ cup) fresh mint leaves,
　tightly packed
6 ounces (¾ cup) crushed ice

Put everything in a blender. Blend at high speed for 20 seconds. Pour into saucer champagne glasses or cocktail glasses. Garnish with the tip of a mint sprig (3 or 4 leaves on a short stem), placed in center of drink (pictured). Serves two.

The Missionary's Downfall recipe that was recently given to us by the family of Hank Riddle, who worked at several Don The Beachcomber's restaurants from the 1940s through the 1980s (chiefly Hollywood and Palm Springs), is much better than the one we printed in the 1998 Grog Log. *We've replaced that one with Hank's.*

By Don The Beachcomber, circa 1940s. The earliest version dates from 1937, making this drink 70 years ahead of its time: only recently has Donn's penchant for building recipes around fresh herbs and produce been rediscovered by contemporary mixologists, exemplified by the "farm-to-glass" cocktail movement on the West Coast.

NAVY GROG

¾ ounce fresh lime juice
¾ ounce white grapefruit juice
¾ ounce soda water
1 ounce honey mix (see page 226)
1 ounce light Puerto Rican rum
1 ounce dark Jamaican rum
1 ounce Demerara rum

Shake vigorously with ice cubes.
Strain into a double old-fashioned
glass with ice-cone around straw (pictured opposite):

Pack a pilsner glass with finely shaved ice, run a chopstick through the middle
to make a hole for the straw, and then gently remove cone from glass. Freeze
cone overnight. When ready to serve, run straw through cone. Sip drink
through straw.

*In 1993 we were living on the beach at Playa Del Rey, California, and hanging
out at a place called the Sampan. Once a posh Chinese restaurant frequented
by flush suburbanites, its clientele had dwindled to a trickle of bikers, surfers, and the
occasional displaced tourist. The owner, a grouchy old guy named Dennis Quan, had
little time for them or us, but one afternoon he made a Navy Grog that was so good, by
the time we finished it we could swear there was a halo over his head. Quan wouldn't
tell us his secret, but when we watched him make our next one, we saw him heat a
teacup full of honey in his toaster oven, then pour a measure of the honey — now in a
more cocktail-friendly liquid state — into his blender. Aha! We'd seen drink recipes calling for honey, but none of them explained how to use the stuff without leaving a sticky,
undissolved clump in your glass. So we happily applied Quan's method to drinks in the
1998 Grog Log, even though having to heat the stuff was inconvenient — as was having to pre-mix it with other ingredients before blending, to avoid it solidifying again on
contact with ice. Four years later, we found a 1950 U.S. Navy charity cookbook to which
Don The Beachcomber had donated this formula: heat equal parts honey and water till
the honey dissolves, then cool it, bottle it, and store it in the fridge, where it will remain
in a liquid state. Voila: easy-to-use honey, available at a moment's notice. We've revised
the Log's Navy Grog recipe to take advantage of this syrup; now you can quickly shake
up your honeyed Grog, instead of having to use heat and a blender.*

*By Don The Beachcomber, circa 1941. Veteran Tiki barman Tony Ramos (see page 130)
taught us the ice-cone trick in the early 1990s.*

Navy Grog

NEVER SAY DIE

¼ ounce unsweetened pineapple juice
½ ounce fresh lime juice
½ ounce orange juice
½ ounce grapefruit juice
½ ounce honey mix (see page 226)
½ ounce light Puerto Rican rum
½ ounce dark Jamaican rum
1 ounce gold Barbados rum
Dash Angostura bitters
4 ounces (½ cup) crushed ice

**Put everything in a blender. Blend
at high speed for 5 seconds. Pour
unstrained into a wine goblet or specialty glass (pictured).**

151 SWIZZLE

½ ounce fresh lime juice
½ ounce sugar syrup
1 ½ ounces 151-proof Demerara rum
    (Lemon Hart or El Dorado)
Dash Angostura bitters
6 drops (1/8 teaspoon) Pernod
8 ounces (1 cup) crushed ice
Freshly ground nutmeg

**Put everything — except nutmeg — in
a blender. Blend at high speed for 5
seconds. Pour unstrained into a metal
cup with a flared top (pictured) or a
pilsner glass, adding more crushed
ice to fill. Dust with nutmeg. Garnish
with a cinnamon stick.**

*Both as served by Tony Ramos at Don The
Beachcomber's, Hollywood, in the 1960s.*

PAGO PAGO

1 ounce orange juice
¾ ounce fresh lime juice
¾ ounce white grapefruit juice
¾ ounce honey mix (see page 226)
1 ounce dark Jamaican rum
Dash Angostura bitters

Shake well with plenty of crushed ice. Pour unstrained into a pilsner glass.

STRIP AND GO NAKED NEW

¾ ounce orange juice
1 ounce fresh lime juice
1 ounce gin
1 ounce vodka
5 ounces lager beer, chilled
¼ ounce grenadine

Stir vigorously with ice cubes until well chilled, then pour unstrained into a double old-fashioned glass.

Dean Short was the Tiki Kahuna of Arizona; in addition to the Islands restaurant in Phoenix, he owned the Pago Pago, Kon-Tiki, and Ports O' Call in Tuscon. These two drinks, both circa 1963, were served in all of Short's places. "A big guy, very pleasant," remembers Leroy Schmaltz of Oceanic Arts, the firm that outfitted Short's restaurants with Polynesian decor. "He had a ranch in this town that he basically owned, in the sense that his property surrounded it. They filmed Oklahoma there. He had these big horse barns, and he had the Tiki stuff from his restaurants stored in the stalls. You'd be going through it and you'd be surprised by horses when they'd snort in the next stall over." Adds Leroy's business partner, Bob Van Oosting: "Dean stole a lot of his drinks from Don The Beachcomber, by hiring away one of Don's bartenders. He got into a lot of trouble for that."

PAINKILLER

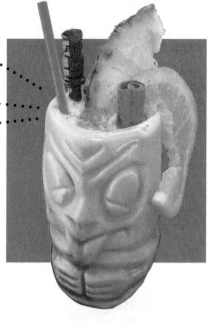

4 ounces unsweetened pineapple juice
1 ounce orange juice
1 ounce Lopez coconut cream
2 ½ ounces Pusser's Navy Rum (or dark
    Jamaican rum)
Powdered cinnamon
Ground nutmeg

Shake juices, Lopez, and rum with plenty of crushed ice. Pour unstrained into a tall glass or Tiki mug. Dust with cinnamon and nutmeg. Garnish with a pineapple stick, cinnamon stick, and orange wheel.

In the 1990s the Pusser's Rum company trademarked the Painkiller, which led us to conclude in the Grog Log *that Pusser's invented it. The Painkiller actually originated at the Soggy Dollar Bar on the island of Jost Van Dyke, in the British Virgin Islands, where*

it's still served today. Our Caribbean correspondent, Brother Cleve, reports: "The Soggy Dollar is a lovely beachfront bar that lacks one major item — a dock. The only way to get to the bar is to jump off your boat and swim. The proprietors, however, have thoughtfully placed a clothesline along the bar for you to hang your soggy dollars out to dry." Adds Cleve, "In the early 2000s the bartenders would often grate Viagra tablets onto the drink, hopefully relieving a different pain, as well as adding an otherworldly blue hue to the concoction."

Invented by George and Marie Myrick of the Soggy Dollar Bar, B.V.I., in 1971. The Soggy Dollar's current owner, Jerry O'Connell, told the Bum that the Myricks originally made the Painkiller with a mix of Mount Gay and Cruzan dark rums. Pusser's is now the official pour, but, since the Painkiller is the only drink in this book that calls for Pusser's, we tried subbing dark Jamaican rum and found that it works just fine.

PIECES OF EIGHT

½ ounce fresh lime juice
1 ½ ounces fresh lemon juice
1 ½ ounces passion fruit syrup (see page 229)
1 ½ ounces light Puerto Rican rum
4 ounces (½ cup) crushed ice

Put everything in a blender. Blend at high speed for 5 seconds and pour unstrained into a tall glass or specialty glass (pictured). Add more crushed ice to fill.

From the Pieces Of Eight restaurant, Marina Del Rey, California, circa 1962. Back then the house band was Paul Page and The Island-Aires, whose numbers included "When Sam Goes Back To Samoa," "Chicken Kona-Kai," and "Big Luau In The Sky," which is where the Pieces Of Eight went in the 1970s.

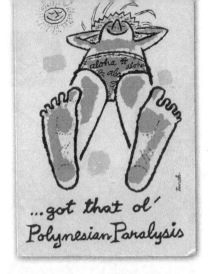

...got that ol' Polynesian Paralysis

HAPPY BUDDHA

4 ounces guava nectar
½ ounce Rose's lime juice cordial
¼ ounce Cointreau
1 ½ ounces okolehao (substitute Bourbon or rye)

Shake well with plenty of crushed ice. Pour into a porcelain Buddha mug, or tall glass.

BUM *Okolehao is a Hawaiian spirit that hasn't been marketed for well over a decade. More's the pity. Distilled from the root of the ti plant, it's a wonderful cocktail ingredient with a unique flavor profile. If you happen to have any sealed vintage souvenir bottles in your Hawaiiana collection (such as those pictured opposite), open them and enjoy — oke is also delicious served neat or on the rocks. In the original* Grog Log *we recommended subbing Martinique rum, but we've since discovered that Bourbon makes a much better replacement.*

POLYNESIAN PARALYSIS

¾ ounce fresh lemon juice
3 ounces orange juice
3 ounces unsweetened pineapple juice
1 ounce orgeat syrup
½ ounce sugar syrup
3 ounces okolehao (substitute Bourbon or rye)
12 ounces (1 ½ cups) crushed ice

Put everything in a blender. Blend for up to 10 seconds. Pour unstrained into a Tiki bowl, adding ice cubes to fill. Garnish with a gardenia.

In his 1960 book Waikiki Beachnik, *H. Allen Smith diagnosed the symptoms of Polynesian Paralysis as "a screaming desire not to work, not to do anything that requires any substantial effort either physical or mental." The most extreme case was that of the Duke Of Windsor, who caught the disease, then known as "Waikiki Pip," in 1920 ... and went on to renounce the throne of England. The Happy Buddha was the house drink at the House Of Hong restaurant's Red Chamber Bar, which advertised "Waikiki's only indoor waterfall presided over by a camphor wood God of Longevity." Both drinks circa 1960s.*

Souvenir okolehao bottles, circa 1960s | Jonpaul Balak

POLYNESIAN SPELL

1 ounce grape juice (the purple stuff)
¾ ounce fresh lemon juice
¼ ounce triple sec
¼ ounce peach brandy
½ teaspoon sugar syrup
1 ½ ounces gin

Shake well with ice cubes. Strain into specialty glass (pictured opposite, center right).

PORT LIGHT

1 ounce fresh lemon juice
½ ounce passion fruit syrup
¼ ounce grenadine
1 ½ ounces Bourbon
8 ounces (1 cup) crushed ice

Put everything in a blender. Blend at high speed for 5 seconds. Pour unstrained into a Port Light glass (pictured opposite, top left), adding more ice to fill.

Both by Sandro Conti (pictured) of the Kahiki, Columbus, Ohio, circa 1961. The Kahiki was a Polynesian supper club built on a monumental scale; the food was nothing to write home about (after eating there you'd be too sick to write anyway), but the decor more than compensated, especially a three-stories-tall Easter Island head fireplace that had to be seen to be believed. The Kahiki was listed on the National Register Of Historic Places, but that didn't stop Walgreen's from bulldozing it and building a drug store on the site in 2000. The fireplace now resides in a back yard in Bellows Falls, Vermont.

PORT LIGHT
Bourbon lovers take this
left turn. 2.80

WIDOW'S WAIL
This potent gin drink   quieteth

KAHIK
This treasure just couldn

NATIVE NECTAR
Nectar of the Tiki Gods laced with blessed rums. 2.80

BAHIA
Light and white rums—listen to the   drums! 2.85

NAVY GR
21 guns! The
standard, an

SATAN'S SIN
Once in a lifetime! 2.65

POLYNESIAN SPELL
Gin laced with brandy will put you "und

MAIDEN'S PRAYER
Barbados rum may be her answer. 1.90

TONGA TALE
Captain Coury had a story
worth repeating. 2.30

This
adver
effects
of the
of F

MAI-TAI
Mai-Tai means "the best"
Special Reserve   with 15-year-old
Jamaican Rum. 3.25

PAGO
Full sails

© POLYNESIAN ENTERPRISES, INC. 1968

Kahiki cocktail menu, 1968

Q.B. COOLER

1 ounce orange juice
½ ounce fresh lime juice
½ ounce honey mix (see page 226)
¼ ounce falernum
1 ounce soda water
1 ounce gold Jamaican rum
1 ounce light Puerto Rican rum
½ ounce Demerara rum
2 dashes Angostura bitters
½ teaspoon ginger syrup (see page 226)
4 ounces crushed ice

Put everything in a blender. Blend at high speed for 5 seconds. Pour un-strained into a double-old fashioned glass. Garnish will several mint sprigs, julep-style (pictured).

Whether or not there's any truth to this story, the above recipe does indeed taste like the Trader's Mai Tai.

We replaced the Q.B. Cooler recipe in the first edition of the Grog Log with this earlier one from 1937, because that's the year Trader Vic first visited Don The Beachcomber's — and allegedly obtained the Beachcomber's Q.B. Cooler recipe, which he later used to create the Mai Tai (see pages 69-71).

Q.B. stands for Quiet Birdmen, a drinking fraternity of aviators founded by seven WWI pilots in 1921. Membership in "Ye Anciente and Secret Order of Quiet Birdmen, about which those who know anything may tell nothing," was by invitation only, and at one time included Charles Lindbergh and several NASA astronauts.

THE LUAU

421 N. RODEO
BEVERLY HILLS

SCORPION BOWL

6 ounces orange juice
4 ounces fresh lemon juice
1 ½ ounces orgeat syrup
6 ounces light Puerto Rican rum
1 ounce brandy
16 ounces (2 cups) crushed ice

Put everything in a blender. Blend for up to 10 seconds. Pour unstrained into a Tiki bowl. Garnish with a gardenia. Serves two to four people.

LUAU SCORPION
NEW

2 ounces orange juice
1 ounce fresh lime juice
1 ounce sugar syrup
2 ounces gold Puerto Rican rum
2 ounces gin
1 ounce brandy or Cognac
¾ ounce orgeat syrup
8 ounces (1 cup) ice

Put everything in a blender. Blend at high speed for 5 seconds. Pour unstrained into a Tiki bowl, adding ice cubes to fill. Garnish with a gardenia. Serves two.

The first recipe above is the standard Trader Vic's version. The Luau Scorpion, From the Luau in Beverly Hills (see page 139), dates from 1958; it bears little resemblance to Vic's original, but oh, what a lovely sting!

Scorpion

A South Seas concoction of rums, fruit juices and brandy with a whisper of almond bedecked with gardenias and served with long straws.

SIDEWINDER'S FANG

1 ½ ounces fresh lime juice
1 ½ ounces orange juice
1 ½ ounces passion fruit syrup
1 ounce dark Jamaican rum
1 ounce Demerara rum
3 ounces club soda

Shake everything — except club soda — with ice cubes. Pour unstrained into a large snifter. Stir in soda. Add more ice to fill. Garnish with a length of spiral-cut orange peel.

The original recipe from the Lanai in San Mateo, California, called for blending everything with a half cup of crushed ice. But that results in an over-diluted version of an already mild drink; shaking brings the flavors to the fore.

SHARK'S TOOTH

½ ounce fresh lime juice
½ ounce unsweetened pineapple juice
½ ounce sugar syrup
1 ounce gold Barbados rum
1 ounce dark Jamaican rum
Teaspoon syrup from maraschino
    cherry jar
3 ounces crushed ice

Put everything — except Jamaican rum — in a blender. Blend for 5 seconds. Pour unstrained into an old-fashioned glass. Serve Jamaican rum separately in a shot glass, to be poured into the drink. Sip assembled drink without straw.

Midcentury exotica didn't just cater to suburban fantasies of work-free islands and guilt-free sex. There was also the call of adventure, epitomized by these classic "dangerous" drinks: if the sharks didn't eat you, the cannibals would.

SHRUNKEN SKULL

1 ounce fresh lime juice
1 ounce pomegranate syrup or
    grenadine (see page 226)
1 ounce gold Puerto Rican rum
1 ounce Demerara rum

Shake vigorously with ice cubes. Pour unstrained into a skull mug (pictured opposite).

Shrunken Skull | Cass McClure

THE SINGAPORE SLING: RAFFLES BAFFLES DRINK DETECTIVES

Like the Mai Tai, the Singapore Sling has taken a lot of abuse over the years. The current incarnation includes pineapple juice and grenadine; the Raffles Hotel, which claims to be the home of the Singapore Sling, has since the 1970s touted this version as the "authentic" recipe — even though evidence to the contrary abounds. In his book *The Gentleman's Companion*, Charles Baker printed a Raffles Singapore Sling recipe he'd copied down in 1926 (gin, cherry brandy, Bénédictine); in 1957, the vice president of the Overseas Press Club, Lawrence Blochman, offered a vaguely similar Raffles recipe (gin, cherry cordial, Bénédictine, lime juice, bitters) in his book *Here's How! A Round-The-World Bar Guide*.

Blochman, who covered Singapore as a foreign correspondent in the 1920s, also threw cold water on Raffles' proprietary claims. "What has come to be known as the Singapore Sling," he wrote in *Here's How!*, "was originally called the Sandakan Sling, after the Borneo port where it was invented ... the recipe spread to Singapore, where it was quickly adopted by the bartenders of the Raffles, the Europe, the Van Wijk," and other hotels, "each of whom added a dash of this or that and gave it a new name."

In the case of Raffles, bartender Ngiam Tong Boon added his "this or that" between 1905 and 1915, but his exact changes have been lost to time: Ted "Doctor Cocktail" Haigh, who published his extensive Singapore Sling research in 2005 in *The Journal Of The American Cocktail*, reports that after Raffles started getting flak for hyping its pineapple-and-grenadine mutation, the hotel's spokespeople had to admit "not having the original recipe at all."

Doctor Haigh also contraindicates Blochman's Sandakan Sling story. The precursor of the Singapore Sling, suggests the Doctor, is the Straits Sling (gin, kirsch, Bénédictine, lemon juice, Angostura and orange bitters).

Wherever it came from, and however inauthentic it may be, today's pineapple-and-grenadine Singapore Sling is actually a pretty good drink. We've included it below, under two earlier recipes of note.

SINGAPORE SLING (?-1950S)

1 ounce fresh lime juice	½ ounce brandy
1 ounce Cherry Heering	2 ounces gin
½ ounce Bénédictine	1 ½ ounces club soda (or more to taste)

Shake everything — except soda — with ice cubes. Stir in soda. Strain into a tall glass. Add fresh ice to fill. Garnish with an orange wheel and mint sprig (pictured opposite).

We stumbled on this recipe in a midcentury issue of Gourmet *magazine. It appeared in a letter to the editor from a Singapore resident, who chastised the magazine for*

Singapore Sling | Martin Doudoroff

having previously printed an incorrect *Raffles* Hotel recipe. While there's no proof that this "corrected" recipe is definitive either, it tastes better to us than any other version we've tried — and we've tried 'em all.

SINGAPORE SLING (1930S) NEW

½ ounce fresh lemon juice
1 ounce cherry-flavored brandy (use Cherry Heering)
1 ounce gin
1 ½ ounces soda water

Shake gin, cherry brandy, and lemon juice with ice cubes. Stir in soda. Pour unstrained into a tall glass, if necessary adding more ice to fill. Garnish with a mint sprig.

Don The Beachcomber's version, circa 1937. Donn Beach visited the Long Bar of Raffles Hotel in the late 1920s, so his Singapore Sling could be an indication of what Raffles was slinging at the time. On the other hand, it could just be cribbed from Harry Craddock's 1930 Savoy Cocktail Book. *Craddock's Singapore Sling calls for 1 ounce gin and ½ ounce each lemon juice and cherry brandy, topped with soda.*

SINGAPORE SLING (1970S-?) NEW

2 ounces gin
2 ounces unsweetened pineapple juice
¾ ounce fresh lime juice
¾ ounce Cherry Heering
¼ ounce Cointreau
¼ ounce Bénédictine
¼ ounce grenadine
Dash Angostura Bitters
½ ounce Soda water (or more to taste)

Shake everything — except soda — with ice. Stir in soda. Strain into an ice-filled Collins glass. Garnish with a cocktail cherry and slices of orange and pineapple.

The modern Raffles reformulation, greatly improved by Ted "Doctor Cocktail" Haigh — who cut the pineapple juice in half, then upped the lime juice, gin, and cherry brandy. From the Doctor's 2004 book Vintage Spirits And Forgotten Cocktails.

Raffles Singapore ......stands for all the fables of the exotic East

SPINDRIFT

3 ounces orange juice
2 ounces fresh lemon juice
1 ounce passion fruit syrup
¾ ounce sugar syrup
½ teaspoon vanilla extract
2 ounces dark Jamaican rum
1 ½ ounces Demerara rum
1 ounce light Puerto Rican rum
20 ounces (2 ½ cups) crushed ice

Put everything in a blender. Blend for up to 10 seconds. Pour unstrained into a large snifter.

 In 2005 the Spindrift was put on the menu of the Taboo Cove bar, at the Venetian Hotel in Las Vegas. Two months later Taboo Cove closed. We don't know if the Spindrift was directly responsible, but there's no denying that the drink takes a lot of time to make. Here we offer a stripped-down version in the form of the Spindrift, Jr., for which you neither have to crush ice nor break out the blender:

SPINDRIFT, JR. NEW

¾ ounce orange juice
¾ ounce fresh lemon juice
½ ounce passion fruit syrup
¼ ounce vanilla syrup
1 ½ ounces Demerara rum

Shake well with ice cubes. Pour unstrained into a tall glass, if necessary adding more ice to fill.

We based both of these on the Rum Pot, by Trader Vic. Spindrift, 1994; Spindrift, Jr., 2008.

SUFFERING BASTARD

1 ounce gin
1 ounce brandy
½ ounce Rose's lime juice cordial
2 dashes Angostura bitters
4 ounces ginger beer, chilled

Shake everything — except ginger beer — with ice cubes. Stir in ginger beer. Pour unstrained into a double old-fashioned glass. Garnish with an orange slice and mint sprig.

DYING BASTARD
NEW

½ ounce each: gin, brandy, and
    bourbon
½ ounce Rose's lime juice cordial
2 dashes Angostura bitters
4 ounces ginger beer, chilled

Prepare and serve as above.

DEAD BASTARD
NEW

½ ounce each: gin, brandy, bourbon,
    and light rum
½ ounce Rose's lime juice cordial
2 dashes Angostura bitters
4 ounces ginger beer, chilled

Prepare and serve as above.

In the 1998 Grog Log *we wrote that the Suffering Bastard originated in Cairo at Shepheard's Hotel before WWI. We got it half right. The drink was invented at Shepheard's, but by Joe Scialom in 1942. Joe's original recipe, from private papers which his daughter Colette graciously lent the Bum, is printed above for the first time. By 1959 Joe was managing the Marco Polo Club in Manhattan, where he came up with the Dying and Dead Bastards as hangover cures. He spent the next 10 years traveling the world as a mixologist for Hilton International (that's Joe opposite in a 1965 Hilton ad, and at Shepheard's circa 1950). The Bum will devote a long chapter to Joe's life and "lost" recipes in his next book,* Potions Of The Caribbean.*

The original Suffering Bastard is not to be confused with the Trader Vic drink of the same name, which is basically Vic's Mai Tai with an extra ounce of rum.

Joe Scialom

TASMAN SEA

1 ounce fresh lime juice
¾ ounce fresh lemon juice
¼ ounce orange Curacao
1 ounce demerara sugar syrup (see page 225)
1 ounce amber 151-proof Caribbean rum (such as
Cruzan or Bacardi)
½ ounce Lemon Hart 151-proof
Demerara rum
10 ounces (1 ¼ cups) crushed ice

**Put everything in a blender.
Blend for up to 10 seconds.
Pour unstrained into a large snifter or Tiki
vessel (pictured opposite).**

BLACKBEARD'S GHOST

1 ½ ounces orange juice
1 ounce fresh lemon juice
1 ounce falernum
½ ounce apricot brandy
½ ounce Demerara rum (can sub dark Jamaican)
1 ½ ounces light Virgin Islands rum
2 dashes Angostura bitters

**Shake well with ice cubes. Pour unstrained into a double
old-fashioned glass. Garnish with an orange slice speared
to a cocktail cherry with a pirate flag pick.**

 *We've here reformulated the Blackbeard's Ghost to
eliminate the need for industrial sweet & sour mix.*

*Our early 1990s take on two late 1960s tropicals. The Tasman
Sea is a riff on the Lady Love, a drink once served in various
Oahu bars; we rejiggered it to include our favorite rum, 151-
proof Lemon Hart. Blackbeard's Ghost is based on the Pirate
Grog from Blackbeard's Galley restaurant, Newport Beach,
California, which gave up the ghost in the 1980s.*

Tasman Sea | Cass McClure

TEST PILOT

½ ounce fresh lime juice
½ ounce falernum
3 teaspoons Cointreau
1 ½ ounces dark Jamaican rum

¾ ounce light Puerto Rican rum
Dash Angostura bitters
6 drops (1/8 teaspoon) Pernod
1 cup (8 ounces) crushed ice

Put everything in a blender. Blend at high speed for 5 seconds. Pour unstrained into a double old-fashioned glass, adding more crushed ice to fill. Garnish with a cocktail cherry speared to a wooden oyster fork (pictured).

By Don The Beachcomber, circa 1941. As with so many of Donn Beach's originals, rival Polynesian restaurants cloned this drink and gave it a slightly different name. It was known variously as the Jet Pilot, Ace Pilot, Space Pilot, or Astronaut.

THE ANCIENT MARINER

¾ ounce fresh lime juice
½ ounce white grapefruit juice
½ ounce simple syrup

¼ ounce pimento liqueur (see page 230)
1 ounce Demerara rum
1 ounce dark Jamaican rum

Shake well with lots of crushed ice. Pour unstrained into a double old-fashioned glass. Garnish with a mint sprig and scored lime wedge (pictured).

We came up with this one back in 1994. It started as our attempt to re-create the flavor of our favorite Trader Vic's drink, Vic's version of the Navy Grog — which, in turn, used Don The Beachcomber's even earlier version as a starting point (see page 74). But since the recipe Vic printed in a sales pamphlet titled "Passport To Trader Vic's Exotic Cocktails" listed only "Trader Vic Navy Grog Rum" and "Trader Vic Navy Grog Mix," we pretty much had to start from scratch. We called it the Ancient Mariner because by the time we finished with it, that's how old we felt.

Speaking of old, it's hard to believe this drink just turned 15. At least it's enjoying its teen years: last summer it found its way into the 67th edition of the venerable Mr. Boston Official Bartender's Guide, *and onto the cocktail menus of Elletaria in New York and Eastern Standard in Boston. Forgive us for crowing, but we're just so proud of our little Mariner. To think that in a few years, it will legally be old enough to drink itself.*

TRADE WIND COCKTAIL

1 ½ ounces fresh lemon juice
¾ ounce orange Curacao
½ teaspoon sugar syrup
1 ¼ ounces gin
1 egg white (see page 225)

Shake like hell with plenty of ice cubes. Strain into a chilled cocktail glass.

HONOLULU COCKTAIL [NEW]

¼ ounce fresh lemon juice
¼ ounce orange juice
¼ ounce pineapple juice
1 ½ ounces gin
Teaspoon powdered sugar (do not sub granulated)
Dash Angostura bitters

Dissolve sugar in lemon juice, then shake everything with ice cubes. Strain into a chilled cocktail glass.

ROYAL HAWAIIAN COCKTAIL

½ ounce fresh lemon juice
1 ½ ounces unsweetened pineapple juice
1 ½ ounces gin
Teaspoon orgeat syrup

Shake with ice cubes. Strain into a chilled cocktail glass.

Three attempts by Polynesian joints to steer gin drinkers away from Martinis. The first is from the Trade Winds restaurant of Watermill, Long Island, 1959. The jury's still out on whether the Honolulu, circa 1940, is the Union Saloon version cited by Somerset Maugham in his short story "Honolulu." But we do know that on Waikiki in 1948 the Royal Hawaiian was served at both the Royal Hawaiian Hotel and the Moana Hotel. Webley Edwards' then-famous radio program Hawaii Calls, featuring the Singing Surfriders and the Waikiki Maidens, was often broadcast live from the Banyan Court of the Moana; up to 3,000 tourists at a time would pack the courtyard to watch the show.

Trade Wind (top), Royal Hawaiian (left),
Honolulu (center left)

TRADER VIC GROG

1 ounce fresh lemon juice
1 ounce unsweetened pineapple juice
1 ounce passion fruit syrup
2 ounces dark Jamaican rum
Dash Angostura bitters

Shake well with plenty of crushed ice. Pour unstrained into a tulip glass. Garnish with a mint sprig.

TRADER VIC PUNCH

24 lemons
24 oranges
6 ounces orgeat syrup
6 ounces sugar syrup
1 ½ fifths of light Puerto Rican rum (a
        fifth equals one 750 ml bottle)
1 ½ fifths of dark Jamaican rum

Squeeze juices from fruit, saving shells. Mix juices with other ingredients and pour into a large punch bowl filled with ice cubes. Stir vigorously until well chilled, add cut-up sections of fruit shells, and stir in some mint leaves for color. Serves 60.

Both by Trader Vic, circa 1960s.

VIRGIN DRINKS: NO SHEETS TO THE WIND

As the spirits journalist Camper English puts it, "The problem with non-alcoholic drinks is their complete lack of alcohol." Nevertheless, virgin drinks are becoming more and more popular with people. (So we've been told. We've never actually met any of these people, as our social circle consists exclusively of drunken slobs.)

Should you find yourself in the orbit of the alcohol-averse, here are some tropical mocktails you can make for them. They're our own recipes, as we find most standard non-alcoholic tropicals either horribly sweet or just plain horrible. This simply will not stand: If one abstains in order to drive home one's fellow fuddlers, one should be rewarded for making the virgin sacrifice — not have one's palate punished by drinks meant for children.

DESIGNATED DIVER NEW

1 ounce fresh lemon juice
1 ounce orange juice
1 ounce passion fruit purée (see page 229)
¾ ounce vanilla syrup
1 ounce club soda, chilled

Shake juices, passion fruit, and vanilla syrup with ice cubes. Stir in soda. Pour unstrained into a tall glass or Tiki mug (pictured). Garnish with orange and lemon wheels.

By Beachbum Berry, 2008.

LEMON MINT SQUASH NEW

1 ½ ounces lemon-mint syrup*
4 ounces club soda, chilled
Dash Angostura bitters

Pack a tall glass with crushed ice. Add syrup, soda, and bitters. Stir vigorously until well chilled. Garnish with a large sprig of fresh mint.

*LEMON-MINT SYRUP: To make approximately 1 pint, place in a saucepan 1 cup sugar, 1 cup fresh lemon juice, ½ cup water, the grated rind of 4 lemons, and 50 fresh mint leaves. Bring to a simmer over moderate heat. Remove pan from heat and cover. Let syrup stand, covered, for 15 minutes. Strain into a bottle through a fine-mesh wire sieve. Should keep 2 to 4 days in the fridge.

Adapted from a 1976 Gourmet *magazine recipe.*

NADA COLADA

4 ounces pineapple juice
1 ounce Liko Lehua coconut butter*
8 ounces (1 cup) crushed ice

Put everything in a blender and blend at high speed for up to 30 seconds. Pour unstrained into a tall glass or small pineapple mug (pictured).

*LIKO LEHUA COCONUT BUTTER is a different animal from coconut cream, and even from other coconut butters. Unlike the latter, Liko Lehua actually contains dairy butter. It's meant to be spread on toast, but we found that it also makes for an incredibly rich, luscious Colada. And if you're skipping the booze, you need all the lusciousness you can get. (Order from www. LikoLehua.com.)

By Beachbum Berry, 2008. (For an alcoholic Piña Colada, just add 2 ounces light Puerto Rican rum to the above recipe.)

TAILLESS SCORPION

3 ounces orange juice
1 ½ ounces fresh lemon juice
1 ½ ounces unsweetened pineapple juice
¾ ounce orgeat syrup

Shake well with plenty of ice cubes. Pour unstrained into a double old-fashioned glass. Garnish with a gardenia, if available, or a pineapple stick speared to cocktail cherry.

By Beachbum Berry, 2008. (See page 85 for more venomous Scorpions.)

TIKI TEETOTALER

3 ounces unsweetened pineapple juice
¾ ounce grenadine
Teaspoon heavy cream
1 ounce club soda, chilled
3 ounces crushed ice

Put everything — except soda — in a blender. Blend for 10 seconds, then stir in soda. Pour into a tall glass packed with crushed ice. Garnish with a paper parasol stuck to a pineapple wedge on rim of glass.

We based this on the Princess Anne, from the Hawaiian Punch Pavilion (pictured), Sea World, San Diego, circa 1960s.

Beachbum Berry's

Intoxica!

 THE ALL-NEW COMPANION VOLUME
TO BEACHBUM BERRY'S GROG LOG

INTOXICA!

More "lost" exotic drink recipes from

the golden age of the Tiki bar

By Jeff Berry

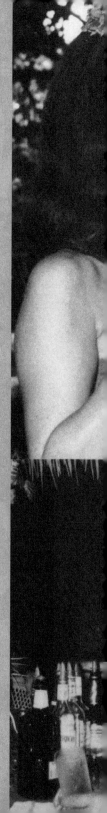

INTRODUCTION

Since the publication of *Beachbum Berry's Grog Log*
four years ago, the late, lamented Tiki bar has un-
dergone a major retro-chic resurrection. Polynesian-
themed nightclubs continue to spring up from coast
to coast, and the trend shows no sign of slowing. Not
that we take credit for this turn of events. In fact, we
steadfastly deny that the *Grog Log* had anything to do
with it. Because if it did, the drinks would surely be
better.

    While reviving tropical decor is no longer a lost
cause, mixing tropical drinks apparently is still a
lost art. The cocktails served in these nouveau Tiki
taverns are on the whole either too sweet and watery,
or too sweet and syrupy, or just plain too sweet.* The
reasons haven't changed much since the golden age of
Tiki ended well-nigh 30 years ago: Preparing a good
exotic cocktail still takes time and a well-stocked
bar — two things most saloon-keepers, old-school or
unschooled, nowadays can ill afford. While there's
not much we can do about the cost of making tropical
drinks today, we *can* unearth the recipes of yesterday
— so that connoisseurs and the casually curious alike
may initiate themselves into the Mixologic Mysteries
Of The Oceanic Arts in the sanctity of their own huts,
and experience the flavors that the poet Don Blanding
described in his ode to Skipper Kent (see page 151)
half a century ago:

> *There are drinks that are mixed by the son of a wizard*
> *to moisten your whistle and tickle your gizzard...*
> *luscious concoctions as mild as a zephyr,*
> *concealing a jolt like the kick of a heifer;*
> *drinks that are smooth as the touch of white satin,*
> *persuasive and smooth as the love of a Latin.*

    Okay, so it's not a cure for cancer, an economi-
cally feasible form of alternative energy, or a diplo-
matic solution to political tensions between emerging
nuclear powers. But if we can get you pleasantly pot-
ted enough to stop worrying about these things for an

• • • • • • • • • •
* Since we wrote this in 2002, the situation has
changed considerably for the better (see Appendix II).

SKIPPER'S DOWNFALL

85c

AS MADE AT 'SKIPPER' KENT'S
SAN FRANCISCO

evening, then we have made some small contribution to the betterment (or at least refreshment) of society.

Thus we humbly present this companion volume to the *Grog Log*. *Intoxica!* is the log of our second voyage of discovery, a four-year expedition in search of sacred texts from a vanished civilization — namely, the recipes from Polynesian restaurants of the mid-20th-century. This time, our ports o' call took us from London to Havana, to Manhattan and San Francisco, to Waikiki and Kuala Lumpur. En route we also collected samples of the best contemporary concoctions, which we have included in these pages, along with a few of our own creations. But the bulk of the formulae that follow are vintage "lost" recipes from the 1930s through the '70s.

Why "lost"? Polynesian restaurants depended on the singularity of their tropical drinks to draw in customers — not to mention draw them away from the competition. These drinks were very profitable novelty items, with a higher markup than any of the food on the menu. The last thing a restaurant owner wanted was for his patrons to be able to make these specialties at home; the next-to-last thing was for professional rivals to poach his secrets for their own bars. Consequently, few recipes found their way into print, and fewer still were divulged by employees to curious customers. The veteran Tiki bartenders we encountered still zealously guarded their taboo knowledge, even the retirees who had no real reason to do so. The secrets they eventually chose to reveal to us resulted in several recipes in this collection. And by combing through decades-old bar manuals, yellowing charity cookbooks, crumbling trade magazines, and tattered pamphlets put out by long-defunct rum companies, we excavated the recipes that somehow *did* manage to

TRADER VIC'S

wend their way into print. Even so, much of what we found has never before been documented in print in any form, including several secret recipes by the legendary "Ambassador Of Rum," Donn Beach, alias Don The Beachcomber.

FROM DONN TO DUSK

In the 1930s, celebrities flocked to Don The Beachcomber's restaurant. Exclusive and expensive, the Beachcomber's was where you went to stargaze — and to sample the novel "rum rhapsodies" that made the first true Tiki bar the talk of *tout* Hollywood. Charlie Chaplin and Groucho Marx were among the regulars who had personally engraved chopsticks kept for them in a glass case in the lobby; driving home after one too many drinks at the Beachcomber's, Howard Hughes caused a scandal when he struck and killed a pedestrian in July of 1936.

Donn Beach's alcoholic inventions outlasted his alcoholic clientele. His Zombie, Navy Grog, Tahitian Rum Punch, Shark's Tooth, Pi Yi, and Doctor Funk, among others, formed the template, credited or not (usually not), for the cocktail menus of virtually every other Polynesian restaurant that followed his over the next 40 years. No small boast, considering that literally thousands of these places thrived during that time.

Besides owing their existence to Donn, midcentury America's countless Bali Hais, Aku-Tiki Rooms, and Kona Koves had something else in common: a collective debt to Trader Vic Bergeron, the second great innovator of the faux-Polynesian cocktail. Vic used lighter rums and less powerful proportions than Donn, no doubt part of the reason the San Francisco flagship of his restaurant chain attracted not the decadent movie stars and debauched business tycoons that flocked to the Beachcomber's, but the cream of Nob Hill society (and even royalty — Queen Elizabeth was a customer). By the end of WWII, Vic had added the Mai Tai, the Scorpion, and the Fog Cutter to the luau lexicon.

In fact, Cuba's Daiquiri and the Jamaican Planter's Punch may very well be the only classic tropical drinks that were actually invented in the tropics — and not behind the bars of Donn and Vic.* Which is not to say that their many imitators and appropriators didn't come up with some memorable variations on a theme. Lucius Beebe, the famously dyspeptic *Gourmet* magazine restaurant critic, wrote in 1962 of "the dismal rash of quasi-Polynesian traps which have now been spawned from coast to coast, making millionaires of third-rate entrepreneurs and ruining the digestions of millions of customers who probably don't deserve any better." But even Beebe had to admit that, "curiously enough, most of these el dumpos run by straw-skirted Borgias give the customers a relatively fair shake at the bar." In particular, the jet-age tourist mecca that was Hawaii in the '60s accounted for many inventive tropicals. You'll find them in these pages.

So without further adieu, as Don Ho used to say, "Suck 'em up!"

• • • • • • • • • •

* We've recently learned that the Doctor Funk, alone among "Polynesian" drinks, does in fact have Polynesian roots (see page 125).

ANKLE BREAKER

1 ounce fresh lemon juice
1 ounce Cherry Heering
1 ounce amber 151-proof rum (such as
    Cruzan, El Dorado, or Bacardi)
½ ounce sugar syrup

**Shake well with crushed ice. Pour
unstrained into a copper tankard or
double old-fashioned glass.**

From the Swamp Fox Room of the Francis Marion Hotel, Charleston, South Carolina, circa 1950s. According to management, Revolutionary War hero General Francis Marion broke his ankle jumping from a second-story window while trying "to escape sober from a party at which this drink was flowing too freely."

What's a Colonial-themed drink doing in a Polynesian-themed book? Turns out the Ankle Breaker is a dead ringer for the Warehouse Barrel Of Rum, the signature Tiki drink of the Warehouse restaurant in California's Marina Del Rey (pictured). The Warehouse opened in the 1960s, so it's not unlikely that the restaurant put its own twist on the Ankle.

BALI BALI

1 ounce fresh lime juice
1 ounce fresh orange juice
1 ounce unsweetened pineapple juice
1 ounce dark Jamaican rum
1 ounce light Virgin Islands rum
1 ounce gin
1 ounce Cognac
½ ounce simple syrup
½ ounce falernum
½ ounce passion fruit syrup

Shake well with ice cubes. Pour unstrained into a tall glass. At the Bali Hai this glass was then placed in a larger glass filled with smoking dry ice (pictured).

SOUTH PACIFIC PUNCH NEW

1 ounce fresh lime juice
1 ounce fresh orange juice
½ ounce passion fruit syrup
½ ounce falernum
2 ounces gold Puerto Rican rum
1 ounce dark Jamaican rum

Shake well with ice cubes. Pour unstrained into a pilsner glass. Garnish with mint sprigs.

From Bali Ha'i At The Beach, New Orleans, circa 1950s, when Elvis Presley was a frequent customer. Owner Harry J. Batt's grandson Jay, who recently found these recipes in the family archives, told the Bum: "My grandfather was a self-educated man. He never got out of the 5th grade. But he had the gift of gab, made friends with a lot of movers and shakers, and he used those connections and saved his money and eventually bought the Lake Pontchartrain amusement park in 1928. He got the idea for building the Bali Ha'i there after seeing the show South Pacific." The restaurant opened in 1952, but Jay's memories of the place begin in the mid-sixties. "In the summer everyone would go to Pontchartrain Beach, but in the winter we sent out what we called Sampans: VW buses with bamboo siding and drivers wearing Hawaiian shirts and leis. These guys would drive into the city, pick up customers from the business district and out-of-towners from hotels, take them to the Bali Hai, and then drive them back after dinner. You could start drinking early — they'd hand you a tropical drink in the van as they picked you up." The Bali Ha'i closed in 1983, when the Batts sold the 55-acre amusement park property to the University Of New Orleans.

phone FAIRVIEW 9859

BALI HA'I
at the beach

STRIKE ON BACK COVER

BEACHBUM'S OWN

¾ ounce fresh lemon juice
¾ ounce unsweetened pineapple juice
¾ ounce orange juice
¾ ounce passion fruit purée (see page 229)
¾ ounce Licor 43
1 ¼ ounces Lemon Hart Demerara rum
1 ½ ounces light Puerto Rican rum

Shake well with plenty of crushed ice. Pour unstrained into a Beachbum Berry mug (pictured opposite) or a double old-fashioned glass.

BUM *When we debuted this drink in* Intoxica!, *the recipe called for 1 ounce of Demerara rum, and passion fruit syrup instead of purée. Try that* version if you find our revised recipe too tart, but these days the Licor 43 provides more than enough sweetness for our taste.

BUM'S RUSH

1 ounce fresh lime juice
1 ounce unfiltered apple juice (the cloudy kind)
1 ounce Bärenjäger
1 ounce triple sec
1 ½ ounces tequila

Shake well with plenty of ice. Pour unstrained into a Beachbum Berry mug (pictured opposite) or tall glass. Garnish with lime wedge.

Both by Beachbum Berry, 1999. We whipped these up to fill the mug of our mug, which was created by Bosko Hrnjak, artist, sculptor, and designer of several contemporary Tiki bars, including the Taboo Cove in Las Vegas and Mister Tiki in San Diego. (Bosko also designed this book's front cover, as well as the covers for our first three.)

We gave quite a few of these mugs away over the years — to our eternal regret, as they're now going for hundreds of dollars on eBay. When it comes to financial affairs, once a bum, always a bum.

Beachbum's Own | Annene Kaye

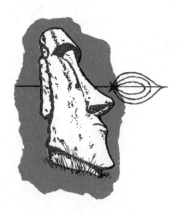

BARBANCOURT RUM CUP

16 ounces (2 cups) fresh lime juice
16 ounces (2 cups) orgeat syrup
3 fifths (3 full 750 ml bottles) Rhum Barbancourt (sub gold Barbados rum)
6 dashes Angostura bitters

Pour everything into a punch bowl filled with ice cubes. Stir to chill. Serves 30.

BLOOD OF THE KAPU TIKI

3 ounces fresh lime juice
3 ounces grapefruit juice
3 ounces orange juice
3 ounces grenadine
3 ounces sugar syrup
10 ounces gold Puerto Rican rum
½ teaspoon Pernod
3 dashes Angostura bitters

Fill a pitcher with crushed ice and add ingredients. Swizzle until a frost appears on the outside of the pitcher. Pour into small glasses or Tiki mugs (pictured opposite), each garnished with orange and lime wheels. Serves 4 to 6.

RUM TROPICAL

32 ounces (1 quart) unsweetened pineapple juice
4 ounces fresh lime juice
2 ounces falernum
1 fifth (a full 750 ml bottle) gold Puerto Rican rum

Pour everything into a punch bowl filled with ice cubes. Stir vigorously. Serves 20.

Three quick and easy punches. In each case, you can multiply ingredients proportionately to serve more guests. Barbancourt Rum Cup and Rum Tropical circa 1960s; Blood Of The Kapu Tiki by Bosko Hrnjak, 1998. (Bosko also designed the mugs in the photo opposite.)

BLUE DRINKS: AN OFF-COLOR JOKE?

Everyone says they hate blue drinks, and everyone orders them. There's just something about neon in a glass that says "I'm on vacation." And it's a myth that you have to take a vacation from taste while drinking them: Technically, a drink with blue Curacao tastes no different from a drink with orange Curacao, since there's no difference between the two liqueurs except their hue.

But there's no denying that most blue drinks suck — probably because all we expect of them is just to sit there and look pretty. Why bother to mix your customers a decent drink if what they really want is something that matches their outfit?

It doesn't help matters that the definitive blue drink is the Blue Hawaii, invented in 1957 by Harry Yee of the Hilton Hawaiian Village (see page 163). It was enormously popular from the get-go, and achieved iconic status when it became the title of a hit Elvis Presley movie. The sad fact of the matter is that the drink is even worse than the film: thin and one-note. (No disrespect to Mr. Yee, who created many great drinks. This just isn't one of them.)

If you are a cocktailian who hates blue drinks, it's probably because the first and only one you ever tried was a Blue Hawaii. Here are some others that might convince you to start working blue:

AQUADISIAC

1 ounce fresh lemon juice
½ ounce blue Curacao

½ ounce orgeat syrup
2 ounces gold Barbados rum

Shake well with ice cubes. Pour unstrained into an old-fashioned glass.

By Beachbum Berry, 2009.

Blue Hawaii (left), The Best Year (center), Marlin (right) | Cass McClure

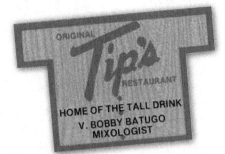

ORIGINAL *Tip's* RESTAURANT

HOME OF THE TALL DRINK
V. BOBBY BATUGO
MIXOLOGIST

THE BEST YEAR **NEW**

3 ounces unsweetened pineapple juice
¾ ounce Licor 43
¾ ounce blue Curacao
¾ ounce Rose's lime juice cordial
2 ¼ ounces vodka
8 ounces (1 cup) crushed ice

Put everything in a blender. Blend for up to 30 seconds. Pour unstrained into a tulip glass or other glass (pictured on previous page), adding more crushed ice to fill. Garnish with a pineapple chunk speared to a cocktail cherry, and a mint sprig.

By V. Bobby Batugo. This drink won the 1975 U.S. Bartender's Guild National Championship for Batugo, the fourth time in a seven year span that he took first prize. Although he specialized in tropical drinks, Batugo worked at a decidedly non-Tiki bar called Tip's, attached to a nondescript coffee shop off the I-5 freeway in Valencia, California. But according to his fellow U.S.B.G. member Bob Esmino, Batugo's influence extended well beyond his home turf. Esmino credits Batugo's prize-winning recipes with introducing Americans to Amaretto, Bailey's, and Midori.

BLUE DOLPHIN **NEW**

1 ounce vodka
1 ounce French vermouth
½ ounce blue Curacao
½ ounce coconut rum

Shake with ice cubes. Strain into a chilled cocktail glass. Garnish with an orange slice on rim of glass.

By Gavin Inglis of the Dolphin Brasserie, London, 1986.

BLUE HAWAII

2 ounces unsweetened pineapple juice
¾ ounce fresh lemon juice
¾ ounce blue Curacao
¼ ounce sugar syrup
½ teaspoon cream or half & half
1 ½ ounces vodka

Shake well with plenty of crushed ice. Pour unstrained into a tall glass.

This is not the original, because we don't like the original. The proportions of this anonymous 1980 knock-off make for a Blue Hawaii with more heft, while the dash of cream not only gives the drink a nice opalescent hue, but a "fuller" mouth-feel.

MARLIN

½ ounce fresh lime juice
½ ounce fresh lemon juice
½ ounce maraschino liqueur
½ ounce orgeat syrup
½ ounce blue Curacao
1 ounce amber Martinique rum
1 ounce light Puerto Rican rum

Shake with ice cubes. Strain into an old-fashioned glass filled with crushed ice. Garnish with green and red maraschino cherries skewered on a marlin swizzle stick (pictured lower right, page 117).

By Clancy Carroll, a Milwaukee-based music journalist, 2000.

VICIOUS VIRGIN #2
NEW

¾ ounce fresh lime juice
1 ½ ounces grapefruit juice
½ ounce orgeat syrup
¼ ounce Blue Curacao
¾ ounce light Puerto Rican rum
¾ ounce tequila

Shake with ice cubes. Strain into a chilled cocktail glass.

From the Pago Pago in Tuscon (see page 77), circa 1960s.

CESAR'S RUM PUNCH

2 ounces fresh lime juice
1 ounce grenadine
Teaspoon sugar syrup
3 drops Angostura bitters
2 ounces Rhum Barbancourt

Shake well with ice cubes and strain into a tall glass filled with crushed ice. Garnish with a pineapple wedge speared to a cocktail cherry and lime and orange wheels. Finish it all off with a mint sprig.

Invented in the 1930s by Joseph Cesar of Haiti's Grand Hotel Oloffson. The first Cesar's Punch was on the house, accompanied by the barkeep's warning, "You won't like it here."

A former presidential palace and the oldest resort in Port-Au-Prince, the Oloffson became a glitterati hangout in the 1970s, when regulars Mick Jagger, Jackie Onassis, and Lord Snowden held court at the bar — which was fashioned from a mahogany pool table built by US Marines, who used the hotel as a hospital during their 1915 invasion of the island. A generation earlier, the mid-Victorian gingerbread structure had acquired a reputation as the "Greenwich Village of the Tropics" when Noël Coward, Truman Capote, and James Jones (who got married at the hotel, and had a suite named after him), gravitated there after World War II. Another frequent guest, Graham Greene, used the place as the setting of his novel The Comedians, *in which the Oloffson became the Trianon.*

CHI CHI

5 ounces unsweetened pineapple juice
1 ounce Lopez coconut cream
2 ounces vodka
8 ounces (1 cup) crushed ice

Put everything in a blender. Blend at high speed for 5 seconds. Pour unstrained into a pilsner glass or Tiki mug (pictured). Garnish with a cocktail cherry speared to a pineapple chunk.

MACADAMIA NUT CHI CHI

8 ounces unsweetened pineapple juice
2 ounces Lopez coconut cream
4 ounces vodka
2 ½ ounces macadamia nut liqueur

Put everything in a blender and fill blender to the top with ice cubes. Blend until slushy. Serves 2.

"Chi Chi" is pidgin for "breast milk." The drink is basically a Piña Colada with vodka instead of rum. The first recipe above is from the Don The Beachcomber's in St. Paul, Minnesota; the (far more interesting) macadamia nut version is a Hawaiian concoction. Both circa 1960s.

CINERAMA LUAU PUNCH

8 ounces (1 cup) fresh lemon juice
8 ounces fresh lime juice
8 ounces orange juice
8 ounces unsweetened pineapple juice
2 ounces orange Curacao
½ bottle (13 ounces) white wine
1 ½ bottles (38 ounces) gold Jamaican
rum

Mix everything in a punch bowl filled with ice cubes until well chilled. Serves 12.

Created for the release of the film Cinerama South Seas Adventure, 1958. This wide-screen, stereophonic sound, semi-documentary tour of the Pacific, filmed in the three-camera Cinerama process, was narrated by Orson Welles and featured a cameo by Don The Beachcomber "as himself." The souvenir program notes enthused: "From a Cinerama theatre seat you escape into the 'reality' created by the marvel of the deeply curved

screen and the intense luminous glow of the triple projectors. Hawaii, Tahiti, Fiji, Tonga, New Hebrides — and down-under through New Zealand and Australia — YOU ARE THERE!" Not anymore we ain't: Cinerama South Seas Adventure is now believed to be a "lost" film, with no known prints in existence. Oh, well. At least we still have the punch.

COCOANUT GROVE COOLER
NEW

¾ ounce fresh lemon juice
¾ ounce unsweetened pineapple juice
¾ ounce orange juice
¾ ounce orange Curacao
1 ½ ounces blended whiskey (such as Cutty Sark)
3 teaspoons passion fruit nectar or juice
3 teaspoons grenadine
½ teaspoon orgeat syrup
8 ounces (1 cup) crushed ice

Put everything in a blender. Blend for up to 10 seconds. Pour unstrained into a specialty glass (pictured) or tall glass, if necessary adding more ice to fill. Garnish with an orange slice, red and green cocktail cherries, and a mint sprig.

COCOANUT GROVE COCKTAIL

1 ounce fresh lime juice
½ ounce Lopez coconut cream
½ ounce orange Curacao
2 ounces light Puerto Rican rum
8 ounces (1 cup) crushed ice

Put everything in a blender. Blend for 60 seconds, or until smooth. Pour into cocktail or saucer champagne glasses. Serves two.

The Cocoanut Grove Cocktail dates from the late 1940s, while the Cooler won first prize for creator Tom Stenger in the 1962 National Barmaster's Mixed Drink Contest.

Both drinks hail from the Ambassador Hotel's Cocoanut Grove nightclub in Los Angeles. The 1,000 seat ballroom opened in 1921, when it was decorated with fake palm trees taken from the set of Rudolph Valentino's The Sheik. Papier-mâché coconuts and stuffed monkeys with light-bulb eyes hung from the palms, under which performed Fanny Brice, W.C. Fields, Judy Garland, and Sammy Davis Jr. — who in 1970 revitalized the aging L.A. landmark by renaming it "The Now Grove" and sharing the stage with Sonny & Cher. When the Ambassador shut down in 1989, so did the Grove.

The World-famous
COCOANUT GROVE
THE LOS ANGELES
Ambassador
Close Cover Before Striking

COCONUT KALLALOO

1 ounce fresh lime juice
1 ounce Lopez coconut cream
2 ½ ounces amber Virgin Islands rum
8 ounces (1 cup) crushed ice

Put everything in a blender. Blend until smooth. Serve in a coconut shell or mug.

TRADEWINDS

4 ounces fresh lemon juice
3 ounces Lopez coconut cream
3 ounces apricot brandy
3 ounces light Puerto Rican rum
3 ounces dark Jamaican rum

Put everything in a blender and fill blender to the top with ice cubes. Blend until slushy. Serves 2 to 4.

Two Caribbean recipes that make good use of coconut cream, both circa 1970s.

DOCTOR FUNK

¾ ounce fresh lime juice
½ ounce pomegranate syrup (see
    page 230)
Teaspoon Pernod
1 ½ ounces light Puerto Rican rum
1 ounce club soda

Shake everything — except soda — with ice cubes, then add soda to the shaker and stir. Pour unstrained into a pilsner glass. If necessary, add more ice to fill.

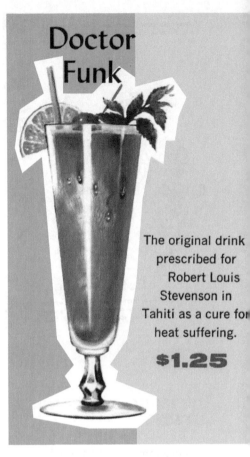

Doctor Funk

The original drink prescribed for Robert Louis Stevenson in Tahiti as a cure for heat suffering.

$1.25

We printed a Doctor Funk recipe from the St. Paul Don The Beachcomber's in the first edition of Intoxica!, *and almost immediately started getting mail from readers who found the drink's three ounces of lime and lemon juice too citrusy. So for this edition we've subbed a variation from the Palm Springs Don The Beachcomber's, circa 1953. We made one change to it, adding the soda water so that you can shake the drink instead of having to use a blender and crushed ice.*

While most "Polynesian-style" tropical drinks were invented in California's Tiki bars, Donn Beach did base the Doctor Funk on an actual South Pacific drink. Robert Louis Stevenson's physician during his last days in Samoa was a German named Bernard Funk. Dr. Funk not only practiced medicine, but mixology. In his 1920 bestseller White Shadows In The South Seas, *Frederick O'Brien wrote of the doctor: "his own fame has spread, not as a healer, but as a dram-decocter, from Samoa to Tahiti. 'Dr. Funk!' one hears in every club and bar. Its particular merits are claimed by experts to be a stiffening of the spine when one is all in; an imparting of courage to live to men worn out by doing nothing." Funk's potion, which O'Brien described as "a stiff drink of absinthe with lemonade or limeade," clearly provided the foundation for the version above.*

GREETINGS! FROM DON THE BEACHCOMBERS WHERE GOOD RUM IS IMMORTALIZED AND DRINKING IS AN ART

Demerara Rum, Limes, and Currant Syrup coiled with aromatic bitters.

Coffee Grog

Fine rums and Kona Coffee blended with wild honey and delicate spices of the Far East.

GOURMET COFFEE GROG

Pot of hot black coffee
4 ounces cream
2 tablespoons brown sugar
2 teaspoons sweet butter
lemon and orange rinds
salt, nutmeg, cinnamon, cloves
6 ounces light rum

Cream 2 teaspoons butter with 2 tablespoons brown sugar and sprinkle with a pinch of salt, nutmeg, cinnamon, and cloves. Put one teaspoon of this mixture, a one-inch strip of lemon and orange rind, and 1 ½ ounces rum into each of 4 six-ounce pre-warmed mugs, and stir well. Then add 1 ounce cream to each mug, fill with hot coffee, and stir to blend. Serve immediately.

FLAMING COFFEE GROG

¾ ounce Lemon Hart 151-proof
    Demerara rum
¼ ounce Grand Marnier
3 teaspoons Lopez coconut cream
Hot black coffee
Lemon and orange rinds
2 whole cloves
Cinnamon stick

In a Pyrex saucepan or the blazing pan of a chafing dish, heat and then ignite cloves, a one-inch strip of lemon and orange rind, Grand Marnier and rum. Fill a pre-heated mug ¾ full of hot coffee, then stir in the coconut cream. Spoon the flaming mixture on top, and garnish with the cinnamon stick.

Two midcentury after-dinner warmers.

Flaming Coffee Grog

FU MANCHU

½ ounce fresh lime Juice
Teaspoon green crème de menthe*
Teaspoon sugar syrup
Teaspoon orange Curacao
½ teaspoon triple sec
1 ounce light rum

Shake with ice cubes. Strain into a chilled sour glass. Garnish with a lime wedge speared to a green cocktail cherry.

*GREEN CRÈME DE MENTHE: A mint-flavored liqueur, also available in a white (clear) version — obviously pointless here, since the *raison d'être* of this drink is its jade color.

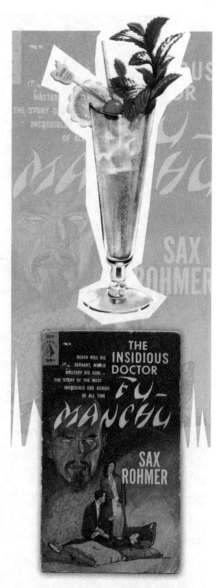

This one's a real head-scratcher. Curacao and triple sec? *Green crème de menthe? (The Beachbum does not wish to speak ill of booze in any form, but ill is exactly what crème de menthe makes him.) Yet the Fu Manchu is not bad at all. Certainly not as villainous as its namesake, the evil genius created by British mystery writer Sax Rohmer. Casually shrugging off charges of xenophobia, Rohmer featured Fu in 14 books published over a span of 46 years, beginning in 1913 with* The Insidious Fu Manchu. *In addition to racist stereotyping, Rohmer also enjoyed Myers's rum. In 1932 he visited the distillery, where, according to his biographer Cay Van Ash, "he spent the pre-luncheon hour helping to invent the Fu Manchu cocktail. This proved rather difficult, for Sax insisted that it ought to be a mysterious shade of green, but, short of dyestuffs, there is not much which will impart such a color to rum. At the fourteenth attempt they did eventually get* it right, but none of them wanted much lunch afterwards."

Van Ash wasn't able to track down Rohmer's recipe, but other mixologists later had a go at creating a Fu Manchu. Of the many vintage versions we've tried, the 1947 one above makes the least sense but tastes the best. Another fiendish plot by its namesake?

GOLDEN DREAM
NEW

1 ½ ounces fresh orange juice
1 ounce Galliano
¾ ounce Cointreau
¾ ounce heavy cream
6 ounces (¾ cup) crushed ice

Put everything in a blender. Blend until smooth. Strain through a fine-mesh wire sieve into a chilled cocktail glass.

GOLDEN WAVE

1 ounce unsweetened pineapple juice
¾ ounce fresh lemon juice
½ ounce triple sec
½ ounce falernum
1 ounce light Puerto Rican rum
6 ounces (¾ cup) crushed ice

Put everything in a blender. Blend at high speed for 5 seconds. Pour unstrained into a tulip glass. If necessary, add ice to fill. Garnish with a pineapple spear and an orchid.

Two award-winning exotics. Jose "Joe" Yatco won first prize at the 1969 International Bartenders' Guild competition, held in Spain, with the Golden Wave. Joe was then the head bartender of the China Trader restaurant in Burbank (see page 130). The Golden Dream nabbed a 1959 United Kingdom Bartender's Guild prize for Leroy Sharon, who worked in the Porpoise Room cocktail lounge (pictured) at Marineland Of The Pacific. Perched high on a Palos Verdes cliff overlooking Catalina Island, Marineland was California's first theme park, predating Disneyland by a year. The "oceanarium" closed in the '80s, unable to compete with San Diego's more touristy Sea World. After winning a decades-long battle with environmentalists, condo developers recently gave the 90-acre site a bad case of architectural acne.

HAWAIIAN EYE

½ ounce fresh lime juice
½ ounce falernum
½ ounce sugar syrup
½ ounce light Hawaiian rum (or sub
   light Puerto Rican rum)
1 ounce gold Puerto Rican rum
8 ounces (1 cup) crushed ice

Put everything in a blender. Blend at high speed for 5 seconds. Pour unstrained into a tulip glass or a Hawaiian Eye mug (pictured opposite).

RANGOON GIMLET

1 ounce fresh lime juice
2 ounces sugar syrup
3 ounces vodka or gin
2 dashes Angostura bitters
16 ounces (2 cups) crushed ice

Put everything in a blender. Blend at high speed for 20 seconds, or until frappéd. Pour unstrained into two cocktail glasses, piling up the frozen mixture as you go (pictured). Garnish with a green cocktail cherry.

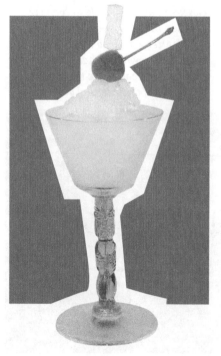

Both as served by Tony Ramos of the China Trader restaurant in Burbank, California, 1963. Lee Marvin, Bob Hope, and Jack Webb were regulars, along with a steady stream of contract players from the Warner Brothers Studios down the street — including the cast of the 1959-63 TV series Hawaiian Eye. *Set at the Hawaiian Village Hotel on Waikiki (see page 163), the show starred Robert Conrad as a hotel detective, Poncie Ponce as a ukulele-playing cab driver, and Connie Stevens as Cricket, the "singing photographer" who performed nightly at the Village's Shell Bar. Tony Ramos created the Hawaiian Eye especially for the trio, who would take over the China Trader bar four to five nights a week after filming interior scenes on the Warners lot; unmoved by the honor, Conrad stuck to his usual China Trader tipple, the Rangoon Gimlet.*

Hawaiian Eye | Kevin Kidney

SCHOONER

1 ounce fresh lime juice
1 ounce fresh lemon juice
1 ounce sugar syrup
1 ½ ounces papaya nectar
2 ounces Port wine
½ ounce light Puerto Rican rum
½ ounce 151-proof Caribbean rum
    (Cruzan or Bacardi)

Shake well with crushed ice. Pour unstrained into a double old-fashioned glass, if necessary adding more ice to fill.

JAGUAR

1 ounce fresh lime juice
2 ounces dark Jamaican rum
2 ounces champagne
¼ ounce Cognac
¼ ounce orgeat syrup
¼ ounce sugar syrup
Teaspoon sloe gin
Teaspoon Cointreau
Teaspoon crème de cacao
Teaspoon Port wine
Teaspoon Italian vermouth

Pour everything — except champagne — into a tall frosted glass packed with crushed ice. Stir to chill. Top with champagne. Garnish with a long sliver of fresh pineapple, stuck with four picks with a cocktail cherry on each.

Two tropicals incorporating Port, both from Seattle restaurants. Art Sampson of The Colony created the Jaguar circa 1955, roughly the same time that the Four Winds served the Schooner. (The Four Winds was located inside a retired Puget Sound ferryboat, atop whose pilothouse stood a 24-foot-tall pirate beckoning customers inside.)

JUNGLE BIRD

¾ ounce Campari
½ ounce fresh lime juice
½ ounce sugar syrup
4 ounces unsweetened pineapple juice
1 ½ ounces dark Jamaican rum

Shake well with plenty of ice cubes. Pour unstrained into a double old-fashioned glass. Garnish with an or-chid, and a cocktail cherry speared to lemon and orange wheels.

PARADISE COOLER **NEW**

1 ounce orange juice
½ ounce fresh lime juice
½ ounce falernum
¼ ounce Cherry Heering
1 ounce light rum

Shake well with crushed ice. Pour unstrained into a tall glass, if necessary adding more ice to fill. Garnish with a cocktail cherry speared to a thin apple wedge. Top off with a sprig of fresh mint.

Two from the Hilton hotel chain. The Jungle Bird perched at the Aviary Bar of the Kuala Lumpur Hilton, circa 1978; the Paradise Cooler is from the Denver Hilton, circa 1960.

kava bowl

My original Kava bowl, before the white man came, was a heady potion. Now I blend light and dark rums in place of okolehao — I think you'll enjoy it.

THE ROYAL HAWAIIAN HOTEL · ON

high chief menehune says "okole maluna." TRADER VIC'S

KAVA BOWL

4 ounces fresh lemon juice
2 ounces unsweetened pineapple juice
1 ounce grenadine
1 ounce orgeat syrup
1 ounce Rhum Barbancourt
6 ounces light Puerto Rican rum
18 ounces (2 ¼ cups) crushed ice

Put everything in a blender. Blend for up to 20 seconds. Pour unstrained into a Tiki bowl, adding ice cubes to fill (pictured opposite). Garnish with a gardenia and serve with long straws. Serves 4.

RUM KEG

4 ounces fresh lemon juice
2 ounces unsweetened pineapple juice
1 ounce apricot brandy
1 ounce passion fruit syrup
1 ounce sugar syrup
1 ounce dark Jamaican rum
5 ounces light Puerto Rican rum
16 ounces (2 cups) crushed ice

Put everything in a blender. Blend for up to 20 seconds. Pour unstrained into a communal rum keg or into individual barrel mugs. Add ice cubes to fill. Serves 2 to 4.

Two communal drinks by Trader Vic. Kava Bowl circa 1940s, Rum Keg 1950s.

Kava Bowl

MARA-AMU

¾ ounce fresh lime juice
¾ ounce fresh orange juice
¾ ounce white grapefruit juice
¾ ounce passion fruit syrup
½ ounce light Puerto Rican rum
½ ounce gold Puerto Rican rum
½ ounce dark Jamaican rum
1 cup (8 ounces) crushed ice

Put everything into a blender and blend at high speed for exactly 5 seconds. Pour into a tall glass or Mara-Amu mug (pictured opposite, upper right).

By Mariano Licudine (pictured) of the Mai-Kai restaurant, Fort Lauderdale, Florida, circa 1970s. The Mai-Kai, which opened in 1956 and recently celebrated its 50th anniversary, is the last perfectly preserved example of a midcentury Polynesian Pop showplace, complete with indoor waterfalls, tropical jungle gardens, nautical-themed restrooms, live Tahitian fire-dancers, and several Tiki-filled dining rooms. As if that's not enough, the drinks — created by Mariano, who was there from opening day till his retirement in 1980 — are first-rate. Mariano spent 16 years behind the stick at the Chicago Don The Beachcomber's before joining the Mai-Kai, where he tweaked Donn's recipes and added many of his own. The Mara-Amu is a streamlined version of an earlier drink he invented called the Big Bamboo.

Mariano's Mai-Kai drinks, circa 1970

OAHU GIN SLING

1 ounce fresh lime juice
½ ounce crème de cassis
½ ounce Bénédictine
Teaspoon sugar syrup
2 ounces gin
3 ounces club soda, chilled

Shake everything — except soda — with ice cubes, then add soda to the shaker and stir. Pour unstrained into a pilsner glass. If necessary, add more ice to fill. Garnish with a lime spiral, made by cutting a continuous strip of rind peeled from the top to the bottom of a large lime. Place spiral in the glass, hooking it to the rim.

MANGO COOLER

3 ounces mango nectar
1 ½ ounces orange juice
½ ounce fresh lemon juice
½ ounce Cointreau
1 ½ ounces vodka

Shake well with ice cubes. Pour unstrained into a tall glass. Garnish with an orange slice.

Both by Thomas Mario, food and drink editor of Playboy *magazine, circa 1970.*

MARTIKI

1 ½ ounces light Cuban rum (sub Flor de Caña Extra Dry)
½ ounce kümmel*

Stir well with plenty of ice, then strain into a cocktail glass. Garnish with a lemon twist and slice of coconut.

*KÜMMEL. A caraway-flavored liqueur. Gilka is the best brand.

BUM *In the first edition of* Intoxica! *we printed a quite different Martiki recipe calling for a jigger of white rum, a pony of French vermouth, and a dash of orange bitters. This formula was an attempt by an old Luau customer to reconstruct the taste of the drink from memory. But the above recipe is the real thing, exactly as served at the Luau, from the recipe book of former Steve Crane employee Bob Esmino.*

BEVERLY HILLS

From the Luau restaurant, Beverly Hills, California. The menu called this cocktail "our Polynesian answer to the dry Martini." Circa 1953, the year Steve Crane — ex-card shark, ex-actor, and ex-husband of Lana Turner — opened the Luau. "High Talking Chief Stefooma" created a new standard in luxe Tiki decor, filling his restaurant with, as he put it, "square bamboo obtained by forcing the trees to grow through square iron collars, man-eating clams from the Indian Ocean, tables cut from giant Monkey-Pod trees, the trunks of which were brought laboriously out of the Hawaiian hills on the backs of natives," and spears which Crane claimed had bat-wing tips dipped in poison by New Guinea headhunters. Crane's daughter Cheryl later revealed that it was less the elaborate decor than Crane's policy of stocking the bar with glamorous hookers that made the Luau the toast of the local movie colony. In the 1960s, the New Hollywood crowd took over the Luau from old-guard regulars like Clark Gable and Billy Wilder; Jack Nicholson, Steve McQueen, Candace Bergen and Dennis Hopper (who rode up to the valet station on his Harley) plotted their futures in the sought-after booths. ("Booths at the Luau were like wombs," wrote talent manager Jerry Heller in his memoir. "They gave birth to careers.") In 1979 the Luau was demolished to make way for a parking lot, but in 2008 rock promoter Andrew Hewitt opened a new Luau around the corner (see page 182).

MIEHANA

1 ounce fresh lime juice
1 ounce orange juice
1 ounce unsweetened pineapple juice
1 ounce Grand Marnier
1 ounce gold Virgin Islands rum
1 ounce coconut rum

Shake well with ice cubes. Pour unstrained into a tall glass or Miehana mug (pictured opposite). If necessary, add more ice to fill glass. Garnish with an orange wheel, a stick of fresh pineapple, and a purple orchid (if available).

HAI KARATE

1 ounce fresh lime juice
1 ounce unsweetened pineapple juice
1 ounce orange juice
Teaspoon maple syrup (Grade A only)
Dash Angostura bitters
2 ounces gold Virgin Islands rum

Shake well with ice cubes. Pour unstrained into a tall glass (pictured). Garnish with a lime wedge and orange slice speared to a cocktail cherry.

Both by Beachbum Berry, 1999. Miehana, "God Of The Orange Grove," was first conjured in 1996 by artists and urban archeologists Kevin Kidney and Jody Daily, as the logo for their exhibit of Polynesian Pop style in midcentury Orange County. The exhibit was held at the Anaheim Museum (spell "Miehana" backwards and see what you get), and proved so popular that Kevin and Jody designed the Miehana mug as an offering to the deity who'd ensured their success. For something to put in the mug, Kevin asked the Bum for a punch with an orange component — hence the Grand Marnier, which was a bit too familiar a flavor when mixed with the usual rum and citrus, but reacted in an unexpectedly interesting way to the addition of coconut rum. The drink ended up on the menus of the Lucky Tiki in Los Angeles and Islands in San Diego, and saw print in The Wine Buzz *and* New Orleans *magazines.*

Miehana | Kevin Kidney & Jody Daily

MR. BALI HAI

1 ½ ounces unsweetened pineapple juice
1 ounce fresh lemon juice
½ ounce sugar syrup
¾ ounce coffee-flavored brandy
1 ounce light Puerto Rican rum
1 ½ ounces dark Jamaican rum

**Shake with crushed ice. Pour into a
Mr. Bali Hai mug (pictured).**

BUM Since the Bali Hai opened in 1955,
this drink has gone through several incarnations. The recipe we obtained
(from an old scrap of paper tacked to
a bulletin board in the employee break
room) dates from the 1970s, when artificial sweet & sour mix began replacing
fresh lemon juice in tropicals. We've here
rejiggered the recipe to restore the fresh
lemon.

On a March evening 20 years ago, the
Bum and his friend John Shourt drove
from Los Angeles to San Diego for dinner
at the Bali Hai. Back then the restaurant's
signature drink was the Mr. Bali Hai,
which came in a Mr. Bali Hai mug that
was yours to keep. The mug took the form
of a sad-eyed cannibal who had clearly
suffered his share of disappointments in
life. We were both taken with the melancholy man-eater, and resolved to drink as
many Mr. Bali Hais as we could to obtain
as many mugs as we could. After our third
round, John snapped the Polaroid of the
Bum below (that's Mr. Bali Hai #3 in the
foreground). When our waiter questioned
the wisdom of a fourth drink, we replied
that we still didn't have enough mugs.
"If that's what you're doing this for," he
suggested, "why don't you just meet me
downstairs in the bar? I'll sell you a box of
them for two bucks a pop." We took him
up on the offer ... after that fourth round.

By Al Hong of the Waikiki Trader Vic's, which was unaffilated with Vic's mainland restaurants after 1941 — the year Vic sold out to his Hawaiian partners with the agreement that they wouldn't expand beyond the islands and that he wouldn't open a restaurant in Hawaii under the Trader Vic's name. The bad blood between the two groups lasted until Vic's death in 1984. The only explanation we have for the rift is this cryptic quote from Vic's son Lynn Bergeron: "My father was the kind of man who did not belong in a partnership." The Octopus was served in its own fierce-looking octopus mug. "Much more lethal than the Scorpion," warned the menu. "It brings out the many arms of you."

OCTOPUS

1 ½ ounces orange juice
1 ½ ounces passion fruit juice or nectar
1 ½ ounces 151-proof Caribbean rum
    (Cruzan or Bacardi)
1 ½ ounces chilled club soda
Dash Angostura bitters

Mix everything in an Octopus mug (pictured) or large snifter filled with crushed ice. Garnish with a slice of papaya and an orchid.

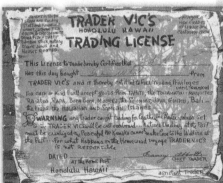

OMAR'S DELIGHT

½ ounce fresh lime juice
½ ounce orange Curacao
1 ½ ounces Southern Comfort*
3 teaspoons fresh lemon juice
½ teaspoon sugar syrup

**Shake with crushed ice. Strain into a
sour glass or small cocktail glass.**

*SOUTHERN COMFORT: A peach-fla-
vored liquor championed by Trader
Vic. We've never been able to figure
out why, because it's never worked
in any drink we've tried it in — except
this one. Available in two strengths;
opt for the 100-proof version, which is
available in small bottles.

*From the Rubaiyat Cocktail Lounge of Omar Khayyam's restaurant, San Francisco,
circa 1939. Admittedly a far cry from Polynesia, legendary restaurateur George
Mardikian's Persian cuisine was no less exotic to midcentury diners who were as
spellbound by stuffed grape leaves as by pupu platters. In the 12th century A.D., Omar
Khayyam himself wrote: "Drink! For you know not whence you came, nor why. Drink!
For you know not why you go, nor where." Some things never change.*

PANORAMA PUNCH

2 ¼ ounces Ocean Spray cranberry
    juice
1 ounce fresh lime juice
4 ½ ounces orange juice
4 ½ ounces light Puerto Rican rum
¾ ounce sugar syrup
8 ounces (1 cup) crushed ice

**Put everything in a blender. Blend
for 10 seconds. Pour unstrained into
two tall glasses, adding ice cubes to
fill and sinking a spent lime shell into
each glass. Serves two.**

*From the Eye Of The Needle restaurant
atop Seattle's Space Needle, where the
drink debuted during the 1962 World's Fair. According to
Western Guest magazine in July of that year, "The potent, lanky cooler is especially good for toasting the 21st
Century or just about anything."*

PANORAMA PUNCH
One of our all-time favorites
We know you'll enjoy this one
Highly recommended!
1.75

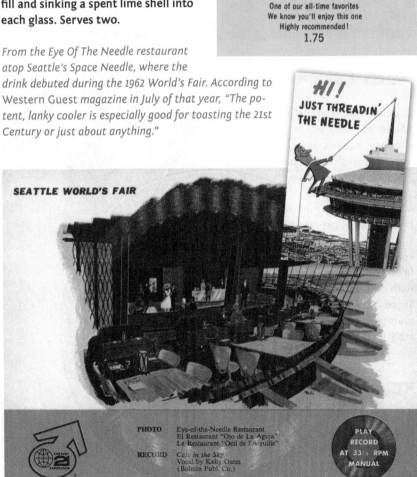

SEATTLE WORLD'S FAIR

HI!
JUST THREADIN'
THE NEEDLE

PHOTO   Eye-of-the-Needle Restaurant
El Restaurant "Ojo de La Aguja"
Le Restaurant "Oeil de l'Aiguille"

RECORD   Café in the Sky
Vocal by Kelly Gates
(Bolmin Publ. Co.)

PLAY
RECORD
AT 33⅓ RPM
MANUAL

PEGLEG PUNCH

30 ounces white grapefruit juice
30 ounces vodka
15 ounces aquavit
10 ounces fresh lemon juice
7 ½ ounces orgeat syrup
5 ounces sugar syrup
A handful of fresh mint leaves
1 fresh lemon, cut into small sections

Pour everything into a punchbowl filled with ice cubes. Stir well. Garnish with mint leaves and lemon slices. Serves 20. (For larger parties, simply multiply all ingredients proportionately.)

Our original Intoxica! *version called for commercially processed sweet & sour mix, which we've here replaced with a 2:1 ratio of fresh lemon juice to sugar syrup.*

By Beachbum Berry, 2002.

PLANTATION DAZE

1 ounce Cognac
1 ounce Galliano
½ ounce fresh lemon juice

Shake with ice cubes. Strain into a chilled saucer champagne glass.

PAGO PAGO COCKTAIL **NEW**

3 squares of fresh pineapple
½ ounce fresh lime juice
½ ounce green Chartreuse*
¼ ounce white crème de cacao
1 ½ ounces gold Puerto Rican rum

Place pineapple, lime juice, Chartreuse and cacao in a cocktail shaker.

Muddle thoroughly. Add rum and ice cubes. Shake well, then strain into a chilled cocktail glass (pictured).

*GREEN CHARTREUSE: A grassy, 110-proof herbal liqueur made by Carthusian monks (who also make a lower-proof yellow Chartreuse that won't work in this drink).

Two interesting faux-Polynesian short hoists. The Pago Pago Cocktail dates from 1940 (no relation to the Pago Pago on page 77). The Plantation Daze hails from the Lagoon Cocktail Terrace of the Coco Palms resort, Kauai, circa 1954. Set in what had once been Queen Kapule's private coconut grove, the Coco Palms served as a location for the movies Blue Hawaii, South Pacific, Pagan Love Song, *and* Naked Paradise. *Maître d'hôtel Walter "Freckles" Smith was famous for his guided boat tours up the nearby Wailua river; Walt Disney sent spies on the tour to steal Freckles' patter for the Disneyland Jungle Boat Cruise attraction.*

THE PLANTER'S PUNCH:
POLYNESIAN POP'S GRANDPOP

While growing up in Louisiana during Prohibition, Donn Beach spent several winters as a crew member on his grandfather's yacht, the Port Of New Orleans, which made rum-running trips to Jamaica. There, at the Patio Bar of the Myrtle Bank Hotel in Kingston, Donn met and fell in love with his soul mate ... the Planter's Punch. The 200-year-old recipe has been passed from generation to generation in rhyme: "One of sour, two of sweet, three of strong, four of weak." This translates to one part lime juice, two parts sugar, three parts Jamaican rum, and four parts water.

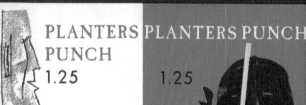

PLANTERS PUNCH
1.25

If you can't go native,
try one [or two] of these instead.

Pedigreed Jamaican Rum, the juice of lime,
then lemon, a few careful drops of grenadine,
a secret portion of red fassionola ... blended
with shaved ice, poured over cracked ice in a tall
cooler glass and garnished with a slice of orange
and a cherry. Delicious!

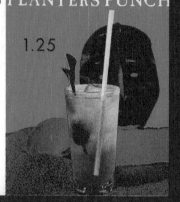

PLANTERS PUNCH
1.25

When it came time to create drinks for his own bar, Donn took this formula and ran with it. Why just lime juice? Why not a combination of lime and grapefruit, or lime and pineapple and orange? And why stop at sugar? Why not experiment with more unexpected sweeteners, like cinnamon syrup, or passion fruit syrup combined with falernum?

Donn took the same tack with rum. To cut the heavy molasses bite of dark Jamaican rum, he might mix it with a dry white rum from Puerto Rico, then add yet another dimension with a dash of smoky, overproof Demerara rum; the result was a complex, layered flavor that no one rum could approach on its own.

But Donn's most ground-breaking improvement was with the "weak." Instead of shaking the sour, sweet, and strong with water, which results in an over-diluted drink, Donn put them in an electric mixer with crushed ice and flash-blended for three to five seconds — just long enough to give the drink a nice chill, but not long enough to liquefy all the ice.

This methodology — multiple modifiers, multiple rums, and flash-blended ice — engendered most of the original rum punch recipes at Don The Beachcomber's, including the Q.B. Cooler (page 84), the Test Pilot (page 96), and Donn's most famous punched-up Planter's, the Zombie (see pages 167-172).

Donn wasn't the only bartist to Tikify the Planter's Punch. Other tropical mixologists took the formula in different directions; we offer a sampling below.

Planter's Punch (center)

PLANTER'S PUNCH  **NEW**

½ ounce fresh lime juice
½ ounce sugar syrup
½ ounce gold Jamaican rum
½ ounce dark Jamaican rum
1 ounce gold Virgin Islands rum
½ teaspoon grenadine
½ teaspoon falernum
2 dashes Angostura bitters
6 ounces (¾ cup) crushed ice

Put everything in a blender. Blend at high speed for no more than 5 sec- onds. **Pour unstrained into a tall glass (pictured page 149). If necessary, add more ice to fill glass.**

By Don The Beachcomber, 1937. Donn Beach had five versions of the Planter's Punch on his 1930s bar menu; this one hews closest to the old Jamaican proportions, but dimensionalizes the "sweet" and "strong" with multiple syrups and rums.

PLANTER'S RUM PUNCH

2 ounces fresh lime juice
1 ounce grapefruit juice
1 ounce gold Puerto Rican rum
1 ounce dark Jamaican rum
1 ounce Rhum Barbancourt
1 ounce honey mix (see page 226)
Teaspoon grenadine
2 dashes Angostura bitters

Shake well with plenty of ice cubes. Pour unstrained into a tall glass. Garnish with a pineapple slice and cocktail cherry.

By Dick Moano, circa 1950s. The Aku-Aku in Las Vegas, the Islander in Beverly Hills, and the Cambodian Room in Palm Springs numbered among Moano's bartending gigs during the heyday of Polynesian Pop.

SKIPPER KENT PLANTER'S PUNCH

1 ½ ounces orange juice
¾ ounce fresh lemon juice
½ ounce white crème de cacao
¾ ounce light Puerto Rican rum
¾ ounce dark Jamaican rum

Shake well with plenty of crushed ice. Pour unstrained into a pilsner glass.

From Skipper Kent's, San Francisco, 1954. A self-described "explorer, lecturer, cinematographer and yachtsman," Frank Kent opened his first restaurant, the Zombie Village in Oakland, to siphon off customers from Trader Vic's original outpost. When the Trader opened a second restaurant in San Francisco, the Skipper dogged him there too, with Skipper Kent's on Columbus Street. The dining rooms housed the Skipper's collection of nautical artifacts, which he donated to a maritime museum in Manchester, England, after retiring to Hawaii's Kona coast in 1972.

RONRICO PLANTER'S NO. 3 NEW

1 ounce fresh lime juice
2 sticks of fresh pineapple
3 teaspoons sugar syrup (or more to taste)
2 ounces gold Puerto Rican rum
Dash Angostura bitters
4 ounces (½ cup) crushed ice
½ ounce 151-proof Puerto Rican rum (float)

Put everything – except 151 rum – into a blender. Blend at high speed until pineapple liquefies (usually around 30 seconds). Pour unstrained into a tall glass filled with ice cubes. Float 151 rum on top of drink. Garnish with a pineapple slice, an orange wheel, and a cocktail cherry.

From the Ronrico rum company, circa 1940s. The interesting thing here is that fresh fruit now accounts for most of the "sweet."

VOLCANO HOUSE HOT BUTTERED RUM

¾ ounce fresh lemon juice
¾ ounce sugar
¼ ounce maraschino liqueur
Hot black tea
Lemon peel twist
3 or 4 cloves
A small piece of butter

Place juice, sugar, liqueur and rum into a pre-heated mug (pictured opposite). Fill with very hot tea. Stir, then float butter. Add lemon twist and cloves.

PUB AND PROW HOT BUTTERED RUM

1 ounce crème de cacao
1 ounce dark Jamaican rum
4 ounces hot water
Pat of butter

Put cacao, rum and butter into a pre-heated 6-ounce mug. Add hot water. Muddle and serve steaming.

The Pub and Prow
901 NO. RUSH ST.
CHICAGO

The traditional hot buttered rum recipe is a bore: just rum, water, butter and a cinnamon stick. But these two toddies, both circa 1950, give an exotic makeover to the old dowager. The Volcano House recipe in particular (created by Bob Ida, then the head bartender at the Volcano House Hotel on the big Island of Hawaii) shows real imagination. The Pub And Prow version hails from the Pub And Prow restaurant in Chicago, established in 1912; the dining room was an exact replica of the deck of the Santa Maria, Christopher Columbus's flagship.

Volcano House Hot Buttered Rum | Cass McClure

PUKA PUNCH

1 ounce fresh lime juice
¾ ounce orange juice
¾ ounce unsweetened pineapple juice
¾ ounce passion fruit syrup
¾ ounce honey mix (see page 226)
¼ ounce falernum
1 ounce light Puerto Rican rum
1 ounce gold Virgin Islands rum
¾ ounce dark Jamaican rum
¾ ounce Lemon Hart 151-proof
    Demerara rum (float)
Dash Angostura bitters
8 ounces (1 cup) crushed ice

Put everything — except Lemon Hart 151 — in a blender. Blend at high speed for 5 seconds. Pour unstrained into a tall glass (pictured). Float Lemon Hart on top of drink. Garnish with a cocktail cherry speared to pineapple and orange slices.

As served at the Tiki-Ti, Los Angeles, in 1961 — the year master mixologist Ray Buhen opened the Ti, after three decades in the employ of L.A.'s most famous Polynesian palaces, including Don The Beachcomber's (Ray was there from the beginning in 1934), the Luau, the Seven Seas, and the China Trader. These places all vanished long ago, and Ray himself passed away in 1999, but the Ti is still thriving under the ownership of Ray's son Mike, and Mike's son Mike (pictured). Open only Wednesday through Saturday, with only 12 seats at the bar, Mike and Mike's tiny Tiki hut is packed with layer upon layer of Hawaiian eye candy. "We have over 40 years of Tiki junk in here," says Mike Sr. "People just keep bringing it." And they keep coming back for the 90 impeccable exotic drinks on the menu. As will you.

RUM BARREL

¾ ounce fresh lime juice
¾ ounce orange juice
¾ ounce unsweetened pineapple juice
¾ ounce passion fruit purée or juice
    (see page 229)
¾ ounce sugar syrup
1 ounce dark Jamaican rum
1 ounce amber 151-proof rum (such as
    Cruzan, El Dorado, or Bacardi)

**Shake well with ice cubes. Pour un-
strained into a ceramic barrel mug
(pictured).**

STEVE'S RUM BARREL [NEW]

¾ ounce fresh lime juice
¾ ounce orange juice
¾ ounce grapefruit juice
¾ ounce unsweetened pineapple juice
½ ounce passion fruit syrup
½ ounce honey mix (see page 226)
2 ounces dark Jamaican rum
2 ounces white Puerto Rican rum
Dash Angostura bitters
6 drops Pernod
3 drops almond extract
4 ounces (½ cup) crushed ice

**Put everything in a blender. Blend at
high speed for 5 seconds. Pour unstrained into a rum barrel. Garnish
with a spiral-cut orange peel. Add ice
cubes to fill.**

*Most Polynesian restaurants had a ver-
sion of the Rum Barrel. The first recipe
above hails from the Ports O' Call in Tuscon, Arizona, circa 1960s (see page 77);
Steve's Rum barrel was introduced to the
menu of Steve Crane's nationwide Kon-
Tiki chain in 1961.*

SATURN

½ ounce fresh lemon juice
½ ounce passion fruit syrup
¼ ounce falernum
¼ ounce orgeat syrup
1 ¼ ounces gin
8 ounces (1 cup) crushed ice

Put everything in a blender. Blend until smooth. Pour unstrained into a pilsner glass.

SKIN DIVER

¾ ounce fresh lemon juice
1 ½ ounces orange juice
1 ½ ounces honey mix (see page 226)
1 ½ ounces gold Puerto Rican rum
¾ ounce Demerara rum
½ ounce heavy cream
2 dashes Angostura bitters
6 drops vanilla extract
8 ounces (1 cup) crushed ice

Put everything in a blender. Blend until smooth. Pour unstrained into a specialty glass (pictured opposite). Garnish with a geranium leaf; serve with straw pierced through leaf.

By J. "Popo" Galsini, 1967. Popo was a short, bald, bespectacled Filipino who inspired awe among his midcentury bartending peers — they speak of him in hushed tones to this day. "If a drink is not perfect," Popo once told the Orange County Register, "I see no reason to serve it to a customer." Asked what makes a perfect drink, he shrugged, "I mix them the way I like them, and I guess other people like them, too."

He worked in many Orange County Polynesian restaurants, from the Outrigger in Laguna to the Kona Kai in Huntington Beach. After winning first place in a 1967 California Bartenders' Guild contest, his Saturn went on to clinch that year's IBA World Cocktail Championship, held in Majorca. Popo had originally named the drink The X-15, after a jet designed by the Douglas Aircraft engineers who drank at the Kona Kai, but he changed the name after a test pilot died in an X-15 crash shortly before Popo left for Majorca.

He crafted the Skin Diver for the Outrigger, basing the drink on Donn Beach's Pearl Diver.

Skin Diver | Cass McClure

SUNDOWNER

1 ounce fresh lemon juice
¾ ounce Galliano
¾ ounce Cointreau
1 ¼ ounces Cognac

Shake well with plenty of crushed ice. Pour unstrained into an old-fashioned glass. Garnish with a lime wheel. (Pictured opposite, far right.)

MOLOKAI MULE
NEW

2 ounces orange juice
1 ounce fresh lime juice
1 ounce orgeat syrup
1 ounce Cognac
1 ounce light Puerto Rican rum
1 ounce Demerara rum

Shake well with ice cubes. Pour into a double old-fashioned glass or Molokai Mule mug (pictured). Garnish with a pineapple stick, mint sprig, and orchid.

Both from Steve Crane's Kon-Tiki restaurant in the Sheraton Waikiki resort, circa 1960s. After the success of Crane's Luau (see page 139), the Sheraton Corporation struck a deal with Crane to design and operate a chain of Polynesian restaurants in their hotels — just as Hilton had done with Trader Vic's. The ensuing Sheraton/Kon-Tiki versus Hilton/Trader Vic's "War Of The Exotic Restaurant Chains" (as a Business Week headline put it) began in 1959 in Portland, spreading to Dallas, Chicago and Boston as Crane opened more Kon-Tikis in Sheraton locations where Vic had already opened his restaurants in Hilton hotels. Vic eventually outlasted the Kon-Tikis, which by the 1980s had shrunk to one lone outpost in the Waikiki Sheraton.

Sundowner (on right)

SVEN-TIKI

1 ounce fresh lime juice
1 ounce orange juice
1 ounce unsweetened pineapple juice
1 ounce pomegranate syrup (see page 230)
1 ounce dark Jamaican rum
2 ounces light Virgin Islands rum
½ ounce club soda

Shake everything – except soda – with ice cubes, then add soda to the shaker and stir. Pour unstrained into a tall glass or a Sven-Tiki mug (pictured opposite). If necessary, add more ice to fill.

TiKI NEWS

OTTO'S GROTTO

4 ounces chilled coffee
¾ ounce coffee liqueur
¾ ounce Licor 43
1 ½ ounces light Virgin Islands rum
¼ ounce heavy cream

Shake everything with plenty of ice. Pour unstrained into a tall glass.

Shaking this one up for the first time in seven years, we opted to cut down the coffee from 5 ounces and not to float the cream (it adds extra body when combined with the other ingredients).

The Bum came up with these in 2002 to honor two pioneers of the current Tiki Revival: Otto Von Stroheim, publisher of the 1995-2001 underground 'zine Tiki News, and Sven "Sven-Tiki" Kirsten, author of The Book Of Tiki *(2000) and* Tiki Modern *(2008) — the Old and New Testaments of Polynesian Pop style.*

Sven-Tiki | Jonpaul Balak

Famous for Cantonese Cuisine
and Original Rum Drinks

DON THE BEACHCOMBER

101 EAST WALTON PLACE

For Reservations — *Call Superior 7-8812*

TAHITIAN RUM PUNCH

½ ounce fresh lime juice
1 ounce grapefruit juice
1 ounce orange juice
1 ounce unsweetened pineapple juice
1 ounce dry white wine
1 ounce gold Jamaican rum
1 ½ ounces light Puerto Rican rum
Teaspoon crème de banana
Teaspoon demerara sugar syrup (see
    page 225)
2 drops vanilla extract

Shake everything with ice cubes. Strain into a pilsner glass filled with crushed ice. Garnish with a mint sprig.

MONTEGO BAY

½ ounce fresh lime juice
½ ounce grapefruit juice
½ ounce honey mix (see page 226)
1 ½ ounces dark Jamaican rum
¼ teaspoon pimento liqueur (see
    page 230)
Dash Angostura bitters
6 drops (1/8 teaspoon) Pernod
3 ounces crushed ice

Put everything in a blender. Blend at high speed for 5 seconds. Pour un-strained into a sour glass.

Both by Don The Beachcomber.

TROPICAL ITCH

8 ounces (1 cup) passion fruit juice or
    nectar
1 ½ ounces amber 151-proof rum (such
    as Cruzan, El Dorado, or Bacardi)
1 ounce dark Jamaican rum
1 ounce Bourbon
½ ounce orange Curacao
2 dashes Angostura bitters

Fill a large hurricane glass with
crushed ice, add all ingredients, and
swizzle until well chilled. Garnish
with a pineapple stick, a mint sprig,
an orchid, and a wooden backscratch-
er (pictured).

*By Harry Yee of the Hawaiian Village
hotel, Waikiki, circa 1957. Shortly after
he started mixing in 1952, Yee became
Head Bartender at the Hawaiian Village,
a position he held for three decades. In
1959 he came up with the idea of garnish-
ing tropical drinks with paper parasols;
what seemed like a good idea at the time
eventually stigmatized exotic cocktails as
"umbrella drinks."*

VOLCANO BOWL

6 ounces grapefruit juice
2 ounces fresh lime juice
¾ ounce maple syrup (Grade A only)
½ ounce sugar syrup
3 ounces Demerara rum
2 ounces gold Jamaican rum
1 ounce gold Puerto Rican rum

Shake with a heaping scoop of crushed ice. Pour unstrained into a Tiki bowl filled with ice cubes (pictured opposite). Serves two to four.

LEI LANI VOLCANO

3 ounces guava nectar
1 ½ ounces unsweetened pineapple
      juice
¾ ounce fresh lime juice
¼ ounce sugar syrup
2 ½ ounces coconut rum

Shake well with ice cubes. Pour unstrained into a ceramic coconut mug (pictured). Garnish with a cocktail cherry speared to an orange slice.

The Lei Lani Volcano is from the Polynesian Village Resort (pictured below) at Walt Disney World, Orlando, circa 1970s, when Don The Beachcomber's in St. Paul served the Volcano Bowl in a vessel with a lava cone rising out of the center. The cone had a reservoir which was filled with flaming 151-proof rum.

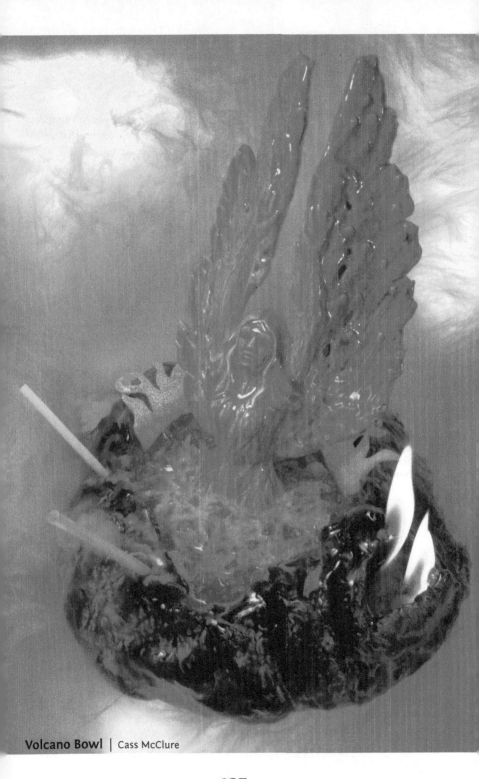

Volcano Bowl | Cass McClure

Stir everything with ice cubes, then strain into a tall glass packed with crushed ice.

Two tequila-tinged tropicals. The Yellow Boxer is by Charles Schumann of the Hemingway Tropical Cocktail Bar, Köln, Germany, 1981; next to the Margarita, this is the Beachbum's favorite tequila drink. Trader Vic featured a "Mexican El Diablo" on his 1947 cocktail menu. ("Go easy on this one because it's tough on your running board," he warned.) The drink disappeared from Trader Vic's by the 1950s, only to reappear in the late 1960s on the cocktail menu of Vic's Mexican restaurant chain, Senor Pico's, where its name was shortened to "El Diablo."

YELLOW BOXER

¾ ounce fresh lemon juice
¾ ounce orange juice
¾ ounce Rose's lime juice cordial
¼ ounce Galliano
1 ¾ ounces tequila

Shake with a scoop of crushed ice. Strain into a tall glass filled with fresh crushed ice.

EL DIABLO

½ ounce fresh lime juice
¾ ounce crème de cassis
1 ½ ounces white tequila
1 ½ to 2 ounces chilled ginger beer (to taste)

SENOR PICO
COCKTAILS

CENTURY CITY • LOS ANGELES
GHIRARDELLI SQUARE • SAN FRANCISCO

THE ZOMBIE: DONN OF THE DEAD

Until the Mai Tai came along, the Zombie was the world's most famous faux-tropical drink. It kick-started the whole Tiki craze, and put Don The Beachcomber's on the map. Donn Beach kept his original 1934 recipe a closely guarded secret — which forced competing Tiki bars to improvise their own versions of the drink, usually long on booze and short on inspiration. Because Donn never revealed his recipe to anyone other than his most trusted staff, over time these inferior Zombie knock-offs became the norm. That's why when you order a Zombie today, you get the cocktail equivalent of pot luck: whatever fruit juices and syrups happen to be behind the bar that night, spiked with an equally indiscriminate mix of cheap rums. Not even a binge-drinking frat boy would risk his fake I.D. on the result.

The Beachbum spent 10 years trying to track down Donn's original Zombie recipe, and when he did, he found that it was partially encoded so that Donn's employees couldn't sell it to his competitors. The Bum could easily write a whole chapter about how he cracked the code. In fact, he did: Chapter Six of *Beachbum Berry's Sippin' Safari* details the history of the drink, and the Bum's quest to quaff the original.

Since you already own that book, we'll skip the backstory here and just cut to the — ... what? You don't own *Sippin' Safari*? Well, go ahead and order it. We'll wait.

All finished? Moving right along then. In addition to Donn's 1934 original and 1950 variation, we've included other Zombies here, including two for the benefit of readers who can't find an essential ingredient in Donn's versions: Lemon Hart 151-proof Demerara rum. In Donn's day there were several brands to choose from (Hudson's Bay, Trower's Gold Lion, and Lownde's were all on offer at Don The Beachcomber's), but as of this writing only Lemon Hart manufactures the right stuff, and their U.S. distribution is spotty.

(El Dorado also makes a 151-proof rum which is technically a Demerara, but lacks the smoky richness of Lemon Hart's. While the 80-proof El Dorado rums are all perfect for vintage tropicals that call for normal-proof Demerara, El Dorado's 151 is closer in body and flavor to Bacardi's, and will not work in the original Zombie. But it'll do just fine in the alternate recipes we've provided.)

Zombie (simplified) | Cass McClure

ice cubes to fill. Garnish with a mint sprig. (Pictured this page.)

*DON'S MIX: 2 parts white grapefruit juice to 1 part cinnamon-infused sugar syrup (see page 223).

By Don The Beachcomber, circa 1934. We found this in the 1937 notebook of Beachcomber's waiter Dick Santiago, who had marked the recipe "old."

ZOMBIE (simplified) **NEW**

¾ ounce fresh lime juice
1 ounce white grapefruit juice
½ ounce cinnamon-infused sugar
    syrup (see page 223)
½ ounce 151-proof amber rum (such as
    Cruzan, El Dorado, or Bacardi)
1 ounce dark Jamaican rum

Shake with ice cubes. Pour unstrained into a tall glass or Zombie mug (pictured opposite), if necessary adding more ice to fill. Garnish with a mint sprig.

Adapted by Beachbum Berry, 2007. While nowhere near as layered and complex, this bare-bones version does approximate the flavor profile of the original ... without sending you on a scavenger hunt for 151-proof Lemon Hart.

ZOMBIE (the original) **NEW**

¾ ounce fresh lime juice
½ ounce Don's mix*
½ ounce falernum
1 ½ ounces gold Puerto Rican rum
1 ½ ounces aged Jamaican rum (such
    as Appleton V/X or Extra)
1 ounce 151-proof Lemon Hart
    Demerara rum
Dash Angostura bitters
6 drops (1/8 teaspoon) Pernod
Teaspoon grenadine
6 ounces (¾ cup) crushed ice

Put everything in a blender. Blend at high speed for no more than 5 seconds. Pour into a chimney glass. Add

ZOMBIE (midcentury version)

1 ounce fresh lime juice
1 ounce fresh lemon juice
1 ounce unsweetened pineapple juice
1 ounce passion fruit syrup
1 ounce light Puerto Rican rum
1 ounce gold Puerto Rican rum
1 ounce Lemon Hart 151-proof
    Demerara rum
Teaspoon demerara sugar syrup (see
    page 225)
Dash Angostura bitters

Shake well with lots of crushed ice.
Pour into a tall glass. Garnish with a
mint sprig. (Pictured above.)

*Attributed to Don The Beachcomber
by Louis Spievak in Spievak's 1950 book,*
Barbecue Chef. *Donn tinkered with his
recipes obsessively, changing them many
times over the years. But this Zombie
differs so markedly from Donn's original
that we suspect he crafted it for the benefit of Spievak's lay readers, as it's much
easier to make. (Killing two exotic birds
with one stone, this version would also
have thrown Donn's professional competitors off the scent.)*

ZOMBIE (South Seas restaurant)

1 ounce orange juice
1 ounce unsweetened pineapple juice
½ ounce fresh lemon juice
½ ounce Italian vermouth
½ ounce orange Curacao
½ ounce light Puerto Rican rum
1 ounce dark Jamaican rum
1 ounce dark 151-proof rum (Goslings or Lemon Hart)

Shake everything — except 151-proof rum — with crushed ice. Pour unstrained into a tall glass. Float 151 on top of drink.

From the South Seas restaurant, Honolulu, circa 1970. Here's a good example of an attempt by Donn's rivals to clone his Zombie. In Hawaii, Donn had no greater rival than Spence Weaver, whose Spencecliff company operated the South Seas and 22 other restaurants on Oahu. "He was very jealous of Donn," says Mick Brownlee, who designed interiors for

both men. "Weaver was always one step behind him. The real difference in them lay in Donn's gracious understanding of the romance of his adopted role."

ZOMBIE (Tonga Room)

1 ounce fresh lime juice
1 ounce passion fruit syrup
½ ounce unsweetened pineapple juice
1 ounce light Puerto Rican rum
½ ounce 151-proof amber rum (such as Cruzan, El Dorado, or Bacardi)
½ ounce dark Jamaican rum

Shake vigorously with crushed ice. Pour unstrained into a tall glass. Garnish with a cocktail cherry speared to a lime slice and pineapple chunk.

This Zombie is similar to Donn's 1950 version — bolstering Spievak's claim of authenticity — but requires no 151-proof Demerara. From the Tonga Room of the Fairmont Hotel, San Francisco, circa 1945. (As of this writing the Tonga Room is still open, complete with an artificial tropical rainstorm every 20 minutes. Well worth a look, but don't order from the Tonga's current cocktail menu unless you're already too drunk to care how far their drinks have devolved.)

"THE ZOMBIE is *not* lemonade"
THEODORE STRAUSS, N. Y. *Times*

You, too, may wonder what a ZOMBIE is made of . . . until you drink it; after that you don't care! As GEORGE ROSS (in the N. Y. *World-Telegram*) said: "It's plenty pah'rful!"

THE **ZOMBIE**

World's Most
**POTENT
POTION**

Only two to a customer. That's all, brother!

AKU AKU

A unique and totally different dining room
where the enchantment of the exotic Polynesian Islands
surrounds you! Hawaiian breakfast! Island-inspired lunch!
Tantalizing dinners! Rare and unusual beverages!

ZOMBIE (Aku-Aku restaurant) NEW

¾ ounce fresh lime Juice
¾ ounce white grapefruit Juice
¾ ounce cinnamon-infused sugar
    syrup see page 223)
¾ ounce dark Jamaican rum
¾ ounce gold Puerto Rican rum
¾ ounce Lemon Hart 151-proof
    Demerara rum
Dash Angostura bitters
½ teaspoon Zombie Mix*
4 ounces crushed ice

**Put everything in a blender. Blend at
high speed for no more than 5 seconds.
Pour into a tall glass, adding more ice
to fill. Garnish with a mint sprig.**

*ZOMBIE MIX: equal parts Pernod,
orange Curacao, falernum and grenadine. (If making a single drink, use 1/8
teaspoon of each ingredient.)

Including a sixth Zombie recipe may
seem like overkill, but isn't overkill what
zombies are all about? This unpublished,
circa 1964 formula was passed along to
us by Wall Street Journal cocktail columnist Eric Felton, who got it from an
ex-employee of the Aku-Aku (late of the
Stardust Hotel in Las Vegas). The recipe
is almost certainly the work of Don The
Beachcomber, whom the Stardust hired
to create the Aku-Aku's cocktail menu
in 1959. We find this Zombie interesting for several reasons: first, how Donn
streamlined the irregular proportions of
his 1930s original so that Aku-Aku's bartenders could assemble the drink faster;
second, how the ingredients remain
essentially unchanged from that first
version; and third, how a few drops each
of Curacao, falernum, grenadine and Pernod make such a huge difference in the
drink. Clearly Donn had learned much in
25 years.

APPENDICES

APPENDIX I:
NEW DRINKS BY THE BUM

Tracking down vintage recipes for the *Grog Log* and *Intoxica!* involved a lot of time and travel (but unfortunately not time travel). So whenever we found a "lost" drink that wasn't satisfying, but had the potential to be, we were disinclined to file it and move on. Instead, we often spent weeks adapting and tweaking such drinks into something worth printing. Without even being aware of it, we were home-schooling ourselves in the building blocks of exotic drinkery. Eventually we even started making drinks from scratch.

At first we took baby steps, sticking closely to the fundamentals of classic Tiki mixology. But lately we've drifted away from these fundamentals — electric

MR **LEMON HART** SAYS:

"HOW TO MAKE RUM DRINKS LIKE A PRO"...

blenders, crushed ice, and multiple ingredients — for the simple reason that blenders, crushed ice, and multiple ingredients are invariably absent from the bars, restaurants, Tiki conventions and cocktail events for which we now find ourselves inventing drinks. Rather than bring a mountain of equipment to Mohammed, we've begun making tropicals that call for standard cocktail shakers, cubed ice, and as little as three ingredients.

These situations also force us into trying new flavors. Left to our own devices, we'd probably make all our drinks with Lemon Hart rum, lime, and honey. But sponsored events require you to use sponsor products, so we sometimes end up mixing with brands that otherwise would never have occurred to us (such as spiced and fruit-flavored rums).

When faced with a challenge, the Bum's first impulse is to shrink from it. But dealing with these constrictions has been instructive: we've learned that when you're cornered, it *is* possible to make a respectable exotic cocktail without access to exotic ingredients, or even the tools of the Tiki drink trade.

But enough palaver. Here, for better or worse, are 23 of the Bum's original recipes, all concocted after the 2002 publication of *Intoxica!* Some hew to the classic Tiki formula, while others don't. With any luck, you'll find something within this spectrum that makes you feel sand between your toes.

BANDICOOT

1 ounce canned coconut milk (Thai
    Kitchen Organic preferred)
1 ounce coffee liqueur
1 ounce macadamia nut liqueur

Shake like hell with ice cubes. Pour
unstrained into an old-fashioned
glass. Garnish with a half-teaspoon
of crushed macadamia nuts mixed
with unsweetened shredded coconut,
floated in center of drink. Serve without straw.

*A little something for after dinner, from
2007.*

BARON SAMEDI

1 ¾ ounces Old New Orleans amber
    rum (sub amber Martinique rum)
¾ ounce fresh lime juice
¼ ounce cinnamon-infused sugar
    syrup (see page 223)
¼ ounce falernum

Shake well with ice cubes. Strain into
a chilled cocktail glass. Garnish with a
gris-gris, lest the Baron come for your
soul.

*We threw this one together for a 2008
"Tiki Happy Hour" at the Old New Orleans rum distillery. Quite a few guests*
*had quite a few too many, and forsook
their cars for cab rides home — cheat-
ing the Baron of his due, and giving our
happy hour a happy ending.*

BUM BARREL

1 ounce fresh lime juice
1 ounce white grapefruit juice
1 ounce orange juice
1 ounce soda water
¾ ounce passion fruit syrup
¾ ounce honey mix (see page 226)
2 ounces dark Jamaican rum
2 ounces gold Virgin Islands rum
Dash Angostura bitters

Shake everything — except soda
— with plenty of ice cubes, then stir
in soda. Pour into a double old-fashioned glass or ceramic barrel mug.

*We make no claim to originality here. It's
simply our version of the Rum Barrel, a
drink invented by Donn Beach and perfected at the Mai-Kai and Steve Crane's
Kon-Tiki chain. In 2007 we cobbled together the things we liked about all three
versions, rebalancing so we could shake
instead of having to use a blender. (This
also makes a good party punch if you
multiply the ingredients by the number
of guests you're expecting, then mix everything together in a punch bowl filled
with ice).*

BEACHNIK

¾ ounce fresh lemon juice
¾ ounce Licor 43
½ ounce Bärenjäger
1 ½ ounces light Puerto Rican rum
8 ounces (1 cup) crushed ice

Put everything in a blender. Blend at high speed for up to 5 seconds. Pour unstrained into a pilsner glass or specialty glass (pictured opposite).

If you're like us, the only time you're not thinking about drinking is when you're actually drinking. So you'll understand when we tell you that we got the idea for the Beachnik while looking at the label of an energy bar flavored with lemon and honey, and coated with vanilla yoghurt. Lemon, honey, vanilla – sounds like a tropical drink to us! After a few failed attempts to turn it into a shaken cocktail, it ended up as a blender drink in 2004.

BURMA SHAVE

2 ounces lychee nut puree (see page 227)
¾ ounce fresh lime juice
¾ ounce canned coconut milk (Thai Kitchen Organic preferred)
½ ounce sugar syrup

2 ounces light Virgin Islands rum
Dash orange bitters

Shake with ice cubes and pour unstrained into a tall glass. Garnish with a stalk of lemongrass, split lengthwise and fanned out to release scent; then float a lime wedge on top of drink. Add a tropical flower if available.

It took us a while to get this one where we wanted it; the bitters clinched it in 2008. Like Lebowski's rug, one dash "really tied the room together."

CAPTAIN VADRNA'S GROG

2 ½ ounces spiced rum
½ ounce white grapefruit juice
¾ ounce fresh lime juice
¾ ounce demerara sugar syrup (see page 225)
Dash Angostura bitters

Shake well with plenty of ice, then pour unstrained into a double old-fashioned glass or Tiki mug. Garnish with a lime wedge speared to a cinnamon stick.

In 2008, internationally acclaimed mixologist Stanislav Vadrna (see Sage Bon Vivant on page 210) flew the Beachbum to Bratislava to talk Tiki with bartenders from Poland, Germany, the Czech Republic, and Slovakia; the Bum came up with this Navy Grog variation as a nod to the seminar's sponsor, Captain Morgan spiced rum.

Beachnik | Jonpaul Balak

its date farms and Coachella grapefruit, so we started there. The two flavors did not disagree with each other, but true consensus was only achieved through the mediation of the Fees bitters, whose unifying cinnamon note gaffed the quaff.

DHARMA BUM

3 ounces Tazo organic chai
    concentrate
3 ounces Silk soy creamer (unflavored)
1 ½ ounces spiced rum

In a saucepan, bring chai and Silk to a boil. Pour into a pre-heated skull mug or other hot drink mug. Stir in the spiced rum, dust with ground nutmeg, and garnish with a cinnamon stick. (Pictured on page 186.)

There ain't much call for hot drinks at the beach. But since the Tiki Revival has spread from the West Coast to colder climes, we've been petitioned for winter warmers. Here's a formula we hit on in 2007.

COACHELLA COOLER

1 ½ ounces Bourbon
1 ounce date syrup*
¾ ounce white grapefruit juice
Dash Fee's Old Fashion bitters

Shake well with ice cubes. Strain into an old-fashioned glass filled with fresh ice. Garnish with a long, thin strip of grapefruit peel, coiled inside the glass.

*DATE SYRUP: Finely chop enough pitted Medjool dates (around ¾ pound) to fill one cup, tightly packed. Place in a saucepan with 2 cups water. Bring to a boil, stirring constantly, then reduce heat to low. Cover and simmer for 20 minutes. Let cool to room temperature. Pour through a fine-mesh wire strainer or double layer of cheesecloth, pressing on solids to release all syrup. Discard solids and store syrup in the fridge, where it'll keep for several days. Shake container before use, as syrup may separate. (Yields one cup.)

2009 saw the release of Pete Moruzzi's book Palm Springs Holiday. *Pete's a Bourbon man, so he asked us to come up with a whiskey drink he could serve at signings. Palm Springs is known for*

FROHITO

4 ounces light Virgin Islands rum
1 ounce fresh lime juice
1 ounce mint syrup*
18 ounces (2 ¼ cups) crushed ice

Pre-chill two good-sized cocktail glasses. Put ¼ ounce mint syrup on the bottom of each glass. Set glasses aside. Blend rum, lime, and crushed ice until frappéd. Carefully pour an equal amount into the two glasses, piling the frappé up in the glass. Top each with an additional ¼ ounce of

Frohito | Annene Kaye

179

mint syrup. Garnish each with small mint sprig. Serves two. (Drink pictured on previous page.)

*MINT SYRUP: Wash 2 bunches of mint sprigs in cold water. Strip leaves from stems, discard stems, and stuff the leaves into an 8-ounce cup until the cup is full and tightly packed. Empty the cup into a saucepan half-full of boiling water. Quickly remove the leaves when they wilt and turn bright green – after 5 seconds or so – and strain them. Next, put them in a blender with 3 ounces sugar syrup and blend until thoroughly liquefied. Strain through a fine wire-mesh sieve, pressing down firmly to extract as much syrup as possible. Discard the solids. Chill syrup in the fridge; it'll keep a few days. Yields 3 ounces, enough for 6 drinks. (Adapted from a 2003 syrup recipe in *Martha Stewart Living* magazine).

Mojitos are great, but a bit ho-hum to serve to guests who expect something more novel when they visit your Tiki bar. So we concocted this semi-frozen, semi-deconstructed Mojito in 2005. A bit of a chore to prepare, but stick a spoon in it and you've also got dessert.

HART OF DARKNESS

½ ounce fresh lime juice
½ ounce passion fruit syrup
½ ounce honey mix (see page 226)
¾ ounce soda water
1 ½ ounces Lemon Hart 151-proof
    Demerara rum
¼ ounce fresh lemon juice
8 ounces (1 cup) crushed ice

Put everything in a blender. Blend at high speed for 5 seconds. Pour into a tall glass. Add ice cubes to fill.

Lemon Hart's 151 Demerara is our favorite rum. There's just one problem: you can't drink much of it without blacking out and waking up the next day in a country where no one can speak your language, but everyone seems very disappointed in you for some reason. So in 2005 we fashioned this drink to keep us from sipping the stuff neat.

IUKA'S GROGG

¾ ounce fresh lime juice
¾ ounce unsweetened pineapple juice
½ ounce passion fruit syrup
¾ ounce dark Jamaican rum
¾ ounce Demerara rum

Shake well with ice cubes. Strain into a chilled cocktail glass.

Made to order for Iuka Grogg of the Mai-kai Gents, to toast the band's 2005 CD "The Wiki Wiki Grog Shop."

KILIKI COOLER

½ ounce fresh lime juice
½ ounce unsweetened pineapple juice
½ ounce orange juice
½ ounce passion fruit syrup
½ ounce coffee syrup (see page 224)
2 ounces Appleton V/X rum

Shake well with ice cubes. Pour unstrained into a double old-fashioned glass. Garnish with lime, orange, and pineapple slices.

Crafted in 2006 for the Florida Hukilau, an annual Tiki convention hosted by Christie "Tiki Kiliki" White.

KON-TINI

¾ ounce fresh lime juice
¾ ounce Domaine De Canton ginger liqueur
¾ ounce falernum
1 ½ ounces light Virgin Islands rum
½ ounce Demerara rum

Shake well with ice cubes. Strain into a cocktail glass. Garnish with a paper-thin slice of white ginger, if available. If not, decorate with a long, thin strip of lime peel.

In the early 1990s we found a mini-bottle of a defunct product called Canton Ginger liqueur, which came in an elaborate cut-glass container. It was a delicate spirit that we thought would be great in cocktails. But before we could test it in one, our paltry 1 ½ ounces were gone. Lo and behold, in 2008 Canton reappeared on the market, in an even cooler bottle shaped like a bamboo stalk.

FORTIFIED FRUIT DRINK, EH?

LUAU COCONUT

1 whole young coconut*
2 ounces fresh coconut water, drained
from the young coconut
½ ounce fresh lime juice
½ ounce unsweetened pineapple juice
1 ounce sugar syrup
1 ounce canned coconut milk (Thai
Kitchen Organic preferred)
1 ounce light Virgin Islands rum
1 ounce gold Virgin Islands rum

Step one: **Remove the top of the coconut with a large, very sharp chef's knife. (Start by shaving the fibrous outer skin from the top of the coconut with light strokes, until you've exposed the crown of the inner shell. With a good whack, dig the heel of your knife into the side of the crown — taking care to keep your free hand well away from the strike zone. You should now easily be able to pry the coconut open.) Drain the coconut water into a container and set aside. Save the empty coconut shell too.** *Step two:* **Pour lime and pineapple juices, sugar syrup, canned coconut milk, both rums, and 2 ounces of the fresh coconut water into a cocktail shaker filled with ice cubes. Shake vigorously. Pour unstrained into the coconut shell. Garnish with a long-handled spoon, for spooning out the soft, jelly-like young coconut meat — delicious after soaking in rum and lime! (Drink pictured opposite.)**

*YOUNG COCONUT: Young coconuts are much easier to deal with than the hard-shelled mature variety. They're not only simpler to open, but they make a good drinking vessel, as the shell sits evenly on a table top. Available in the produce section of most supermarkets.

We created this in 2008 for the reincarnated Luau restaurant in Beverly Hills. Like its storied 1953-79 namesake (see page 139), the new Luau caters to a celebrity crowd — some of whom, such as Warren Beatty and Dennis Hopper, used to hang out at the original Luau. Never in a million years — let alone ten years ago — could we have predicted this turn of events. It's almost enough to revoke our membership in the Pessimist's Club. (Almost: we hear Beatty only drinks wine at the new Luau, while Hopper's been sober for 25 years.)

MARGARITA DEL BUM

1 ½ ounces reposado tequila (we like
Cazadores)
1 ounce fresh lime juice
¾ ounce triple sec
¾ ounce Grand Marnier

Shake everything with ice cubes. Pour unstrained into a salt-rimmed old-fashioned glass (prepared in advance by moistening the rim with a lime wedge, then dipping it in a saucer of kosher salt).

Yeah, we know, there's nothing exotic about a Margarita (although one of its many origin myths has it invented at the Balinese Room in Galveston). The thing is, we really like drinking them. Growing up in L.A., we were practically weaned on them. We were also at the mercy of whatever bar happened to be making them for us, and most of these places showed no mercy at all. We've endured

Luau Coconut | Annene Kaye

We did this for the band Waitiki in 2007, the year they released their album "Rendezvous In Okonkuluku." Waitiki and the Bum later teamed up for an evening of exotic drinks and music called the Beantown Sippin' Safari, held at Boston's Pho Republique nightclub, where the Okonkulukooler was served ... and served ... and served. (Man, that city can drink.) The recipe ended up in the Boston Herald, and we ended up barely escaping with our liver.

sugar-shock from oversweet Margaritas, brain-freeze from slushy Margaritas, and clinical depression from Margaritas composed entirely of tequila and artificial Margarita mix — no triple sec, no salt, and no quarter from management if we raised an objection. After messing around with Tiki drink recipes for a few years, in 2003 we finally felt up to customizing our own Margarita. (We stole the triple sec and Grand Marnier combo from the sole positive contribution to mixology by 1980s chain restaurants, the Cadillac Margarita, which was served with a shooter of Grand Marnier.)

OKONKULUKOOLER

1 ounce unsweetened pineapple juice
¾ ounce fresh lemon juice
½ ounce Chambord
½ ounce dark Jamaican rum
1 ounce light Virgin Islands rum
Dash Angostura bitters

Shake with ice cubes. Strain into a chilled cocktail glass. Garnish with a purple orchid.

PORT SAID

¾ ounce fresh lime juice
1 ounce sesame purée*
2 ½ ounces light Virgin Islands rum
½ teaspoon Bärenjäger
A handful of raw unsalted pistachio nuts, shelled

Using a mortar and pestle, mash the nuts into a fine powder. Moisten the rim of a cocktail glass with your spent lime shell, then thoroughly coat the rim in the pistachio powder. Set glass aside. Place lime juice, sesame purée, rum and Bärenjäger in your cocktail shaker, then shake like hell with plenty of ice cubes. Strain into the prepared glass.

*SESAME PURÉE: Stirring constantly, bring 1 cup sugar, 1 cup water, and ½

cup organic unsalted sesame tahini (we like Woodstock Farms brand) to a boil. Lower heat and simmer for a minute or so, still stirring. Remove from heat, cover, and let cool. Then strain through a fine-mesh wire sieve, working the liquid through the sieve by agitating it with a spoon. You'll be left with a little semi-solid paste in the sieve. Discard that, and bottle the strained purée. It'll keep a few days in the fridge. (If it separates in the bottle, just shake before use.)

Many moons ago we read about ajon-jolí, a sesame-flavored syrup used in the Middle East and Latin America. We couldn't find it anywhere, and rendering sesame seeds into syrup proved beyond our ken. So in 2008 we MacGyvered a purée instead.

RESTLESS NATIVE

1 ½ ounces fresh lime juice
¾ ounce white crème de cacao
2 ounces coconut rum

Shake well with ice cubes. Strain into a chilled cocktail glass. Garnish with a lime peel speared to a slice of coconut.

In 2005, we were leafing through old Gourmet magazines (as we are wont to do) and spotted a 1960s ad for a coconut-chocolate liqueur called Chococo. The liqueur hasn't been made for decades, but we were curious how a drink with a coconut/cacao bent might taste. After several failed attempts to combine white rum with coconut liqueur and crème de cacao, we finally realized that coconut rum would not only provide the coconutiness without the sweetness and heaviness of a liqueur, but would streamline prep-time by collapsing two separate ingredients into one. The recipe has since found its way into Beverage Media magazine and the Mr. Boston Official Bartender's Guide.

SEA OF CORTEZ

1 ounce fresh lime juice
¾ ounce crème de cassis
¼ ounce Grand Marnier
1 ½ ounces white tequila

Shake vigorously with ice cubes. Strain into a cocktail glass. Garnish with a white orchid or other unscented blossom.

Our 2007 adaptation of the Ciro's Special, a midcentury rum cocktail from Ciro's restaurant on the Sunset Strip.

YES, DEAR... STRICTLY BUSINESS!

JACK OWEN

THE BEACH BUMS

The powerful novel of the ardent
sun worshippers, the muscle
men and girls of Waikiki Beach.

A SIGNET BOOK: Complete and Unabridged

followed it up with a pint glass bear-
ing a Shrunken Bum logo. The least the
Beachbum could do was come up with a
drink for it — and as you know, the Bum
always does the least he can do.

STUMBLEBUM

1 ounce unsweetened pineapple juice
¾ ounce macadamia nut liqueur
½ ounce fresh lime juice
½ ounce light Virgin Islands rum
½ ounce gold Virgin Islands rum

**Shake with ice cubes. Strain into
cocktail glass. Garnish with a pineapple chunk speared to a green cocktail
cherry.**

*This started off as a blender drink, but
translated well enough to the cocktail
shaker. If long pulls are more to your
taste, here's the original 2002 version: 1
½ ounces unsweetened pineapple juice, ½
ounce fresh lime juice, 1 ounce macadamia nut liqueur, ¾ ounce each light and
gold Virgin Islands rums, and 6 ounces
(2/3 cup) crushed ice. Blend at high speed
for 10 seconds and pour unstrained into a
pilsner glass; garnish as above.*

SHRUNKEN BUM

1 ounce fresh lemon juice
1 ounce apple juice
1 ounce dark Jamaican rum
¾ ounce amber 151-proof rum (such as
    Cruzan, Bacardi, or El Dorado)
¼ ounce sugar syrup
1/8 level teaspoon powdered cinnamon
8 ounces (1 cup) crushed ice

**Blend everything on high speed for at
least 20 seconds. Pour into a Shrunk-
en Bum glass (pictured opposite) half-
filled with ice cubes.**

*In 2004 our pal Bosko came up with a
Shrunken Bum sculpture in our honor ...
at any rate, we think it was in our honor,
given the sad end to the Bum the piece
envisions (see photo on page 173). Bosko*

Shrunken Bum | Annene Kaye

Whitecap (right), Dharma Bum | Cass McClure

WHITECAP

¾ ounce Lopez coconut cream
1 ounce amber 151-proof rum (such as
     Cruzan, El Dorado, or Bacardi)
½ ounce dark Jamaican rum
¼ ounce light Puerto Rican rum
8 ounces (1 cup) whole milk, boiling
     hot
3 cloves
Ground cinnamon

Place Lopez, rums, and cloves in a
pre-heated specialty mug. Bring milk
to a boil, then pour into mug and stir.
Top with a pinch of ground cinnamon.
Garnish with a cinnamon stick and
serve immediately.

An après-typhoon warmer, 2009.

YELLOW SUBMARINE

1 ½ ounces unsweetened pineapple
     juice
¾ ounce fresh lemon juice
¼ ounce crème de banana
¼ ounce white crème de cacao
¼ ounce sugar syrup
1 ½ ounces gold Virgin Islands rum

**Shake with ice cubes. Pour unstrained
into a tall glass. Add more ice to
fill. Garnish with a pineapple chunk
speared to a green cocktail cherry.**

*From 2002, we think ... the turn of the
century is kind of a blur to us now. Come
to think of it, now is also kind of a blur
to us now.*

APPENDIX II: NEW RECIPES FROM THE TIKI REVIVAL

The Beachbum will never forget the night he discovered the Tonga Hut ... no matter how hard he tries. It was a perfectly preserved 1950s suburban Tiki bar, nestled deep in L.A.'s San Fernando Valley; upon entering, we were soothed by a running waterfall, native wood-carvings, and lots of thatch and bamboo. But there was a disconnect: Everyone in the place was swigging Budweiser and the jukebox was blasting Black Oak Arkansas. The Bum asked the bartender, who was wearing a Guns N' Roses T-shirt, if she could make a Mai Tai. "Sure," she said. "What's in it?" We told her, ending the list of ingredients with "the juice of one lime." Before we could stop her, she threw everything we'd mentioned into a blender — including one intact whole lime, rind and all — and flicked the switch. The lime bounced around like a lotto ball, shedding pieces of skin whenever the blades nicked it. Not wanting to appear ungrateful, the Bum drank the whole thing.

The year was 1988, dark days not just for tropical drinks but for all mixed drinks. Bartending was a lost art, the night version of a day job for AMWs ('80s shorthand for "actress-model-whatever"). For the most part, they were only required to uncork wine and uncap beer; at worst, they might be called on to mix tequila with artificial Margarita mix, vodka with artificial Bloody Mary mix, or rum with artificial Piña Colada mix.

What a difference 20 years makes. Today bartending is once again a respected profession, and the best practitioners of the art have brought us into an era of unprecedented cocktail creativity and connoisseurship. No matter what category today's drink-makers fall into — molecular mixologists, farm-to-glass "bar chefs," or pre-Prohibition classicists — they're beginning to take an interest in Tiki as well. (A rising tide lifts all booze.) Some just want to broaden their horizons, while others are attracted to Tiki's modus operandi of the cocktail as conversation piece — as not just a drink, but a theatrical presentation to discuss around the water cooler at work the next day (a practice in which people who work reportedly engage; we, of course, have no first-hand knowledge of this).

Another change for the better: Unlike the bartists of Tiki's heyday, contemporary mixologists are not shy about revealing their secrets. Almost every high-profile bar owner and tender we hit up for an original exotic recipe got back to us with one. So did some of the country's leading spirits journalists, cocktail columnists, and drink book authors.

In the current blogosphere, Tiki drinks are discussed obsessively by Polynesiacs and cocktailians alike. (Some bloggers fall into both categories — cocktesiacs?) So we also polled these two online communities for their original exotic specialties.

A few of the 43 recipes below are quick and easy, but many call for muddled fruits and herbs, home-made syrups and liqueurs, and other culinary prep work. If you're used to playing around in the kitchen, you'll find making these drinks a lot of fun. If you aren't, the learning curve will be steeper, but odds are you'll end up enjoying the process as much as the finished drink.

ARAWAK COCKTAIL

¼ ounce unsweetened pineapple juice
¼ ounce tamarind juice*
½ ounce French vermouth
2 ounces Bourbon
Dash Angostura bitters

Shake and strain into a chilled cocktail glass. Garnish with a cube of fresh pineapple.

*TAMARIND JUICE: If you don't live in the Caribbean, you might have to settle for canned tamarind "nectar." The Foco brand works best (check Asian markets for it). Goya's doesn't have as much tamarind flavor, but it's still better than Jumex, which you should avoid completely.

Gary Regan created this "tropical variation on the Algonquin" in 2001 for Trotter's bar, Trinidad. The éminence grise of cocktail consultants and spirits journalists, Gary is the author of the influential books The Bartender's Bible *and* The Joy Of Mixology, *and publisher of the online newsletter ardentspirits.com. "Be very careful when you add the tamarind juice," he cautions. "It can overpower the drink."*

ARIKI MAU

Juice of a quarter orange (just under 1 ounce)
3 ounces unsweetened brewed black tea, chilled
½ ounce yerba maté,* chilled
½ ounce Bénédictine
½ ounce Bärenjäger
1 ounce Cruzan Single Barrel Estate rum
2 ounces Bacardi 8 rum

Shake everything with ice cubes. Strain into old-fashioned glasses or small Tiki mugs filled with crushed ice (pictured opposite), or into one large Tiki mug. Twist two broad swathes of fresh orange peel atop each drink. Stir. Garnish with an orange wheel and a rock candy swizzle stick. Makes two normal drinks or one "Tiki Big Gulp."

*YERBA MATÉ: A tea-like beverage brewed from the leaves of a South American holly plant. Widely available in gourmet markets and health-food stores.

Created especially for this book by Ted "Doctor Cocktail" Haigh, 2009. "I wanted to create a hybrid between mysterious Tiki punch drinks and the dryer, more ingredient-identifiable classic libations of the cocktail style," says the Doctor, author of the book Vintage Spirits & Forgotten Cocktails, *columnist for* Imbibe *magazine, and curator of the Museum Of The American Cocktail. "I also wanted to reflect something of the real history of rum's use in mixed drinks. To me, that said tea. In some countries tea and rum were inseparable. I also wanted to reproduce the smoky char-*

Ariki Mau | Cass McClure

acter of the early rum. The Bénédictine aided in this, but the yerba maté really sent it over the top. I also invoked the Tiki ethic of blending different rums: I took two dry rums, pulled the vanilla out of the Bacardi, and the spicy oak out of the Cruzan. I let the honey flavor of the Bärenjäger supply sweetness, since using honey was another intrinsic touchstone of Tiki. But the real mood enhancer here was the orange oil from the two peels. It's Tiki, comforting, and Colonial all at the same time." As you can see, Doctor Cocktail does not take mixology lightly. Doc was also something of a mentor for the Bum in the early 1990s. In those days Doc would routinely enter bars carrying a stack of ancient cocktail books, plunk them down on the counter, and demand that the bartender make obscure recipes from them. This being Los Angeles, the bartender was either an actor between commercials or a biker between arrests; depending on his level of interest, indifference, or outright hostility, the evening could be a real white-knuckle ride. While going out drinking with Doc was an experience not for the faint of heart, in a few cases he actually did succeed in turning a moonlighting felon into a motivated drink-maker.

BEACHBUM

¾ ounce fresh lime juice
1 ounce fresh pineapple juice*
½ ounce Rothman & Winter apricot brandy
½ ounce orgeat syrup
1 ounce light Flor de Caña Extra Dry rum
1 ounce gold Barbados rum

Shake with ice cubes. Strain into a glass filled with fresh ice. Garnish with a cocktail cherry and orange slice speared to a paper parasol.

*FRESH PINEAPPLE JUICE: Cut some fresh pineapple into chunks and muddle thoroughly, extracting all juice. Strain. Discard the solids and chill the juice.

How do you get your recipe published in this section? Easy. Name a drink after us. According to the cocktail menu of PDT, a haute Manhattan speakeasy, beverage manager John Deragon "created this riff on the Mai Tai and named it after Jeff 'Beachbum' Berry, a cocktail book author who has almost single handedly brought Tiki drinks and culture back to the future." Aw, shucks. After that, we'd print John's recipe if it were a Jäger shooter. "We'd just started juicing our own fresh pineapple juice daily, and I was in the middle of a love affair with Rothman & Winter's apricot brandy," John told the Bum *when asked how the drink came about. "Mixing the light and dark rums gave it the right amount of complexity, and adding the apricot dried the mixture out without adding too much sweetness. Add a Tiki garnish and people were happy."*

BEACHBUM'S ARRIVAL

25 ml (5/6 ounce) Damoiseau Agricole
   rhum gold*
25 ml (5/6 ounce) Bacardi 8 rum
25 ml (5/6 ounce) Wray & Nephew
   Overproof rum
25 ml (5/6 ounce) fresh lime juice
50 ml (1 2/3 ounces) lychee juice
12.5 ml (a hair under ½ ounce) coconut
   rum
10 ml (1/3 ounce) orgeat syrup
Wedge of fresh pineapple
Demerara sugar

Shake rums, lime, lychee, and orgeat with ice cubes. Strain into a Tiki mug filled with fresh ice. Dredge the pineapple wedge in sugar, place in a small saucepan, and douse with flaming 151 rum. Flambé until the sugared pineapple is caramelized, then drop it into the drink.

*DAMOISEAU: A sugar-cane rum from Guadeloupe. If you can't find it, sub gold Rhum St. James or Clement VSOP.

By Ian Burrell, owner of Cotton's Rum Shack, London, England. They call Ian "The Rum Ambassador" for good reason: not only does his restaurant bar stock a dizzying array of rums (250 at last count), he also produces the UK Rumfest, an annual convention that brings together rum distillers and rum drink-ers, tropical entertainers and tropical mixologists — among whom Ian belongs in the first rank. Witness the Beachbum's Arrival, improvised from scratch in under a minute when the Bum visited Cotton's during the 2009 Rumfest.

CACTUS FLOWER

¾ ounce fresh lime juice
1 ounce prickly pear purée*
1 ounce fresh orange juice
1 ounce unsweetened pineapple juice
½ ounce simple syrup
½ ounce orange Curaçao
1 ½ ounces Cruzan Single Barrel Estate
   rum
1 ounce Cruzan light rum
¼ ounce Cruzan Black Strap rum
2 dashes Angostura bitters
1 ounce club soda

Shake everything — except club soda — with ice cubes. Strain into a double old-fashioned glass filled with crushed ice. Add club soda and stir. Garnish with an orange slice and cactus-shaped swizzle stick.

*PRICKLY PEAR: Available frozen, but many supermarkets stock fresh prickly pear, sometimes labeled "cactus pear." To purée one, peel off the outer lay-

that groovy Quincy Jones Cactus Flower movie soundtrack."

COFFEE SYRUP

1 cup of medium-roast coffee beans
2 cups brandy
1 ½ cups brown sugar
1 ½ cups water

Step one: **Crack all the coffee beans, then place in a jar with the brandy. Seal it and let sit for three to four days, then strain the brandy.** *Step two:* **Make a brown sugar syrup by heating the sugar and water until sugar dissolves. Let cool, then combine the syrup with your coffee-infused brandy.**

ers of skin, cut off the top and bottom knobs, and place the soft reddish fruit in a bowl. Thoroughly crush the fruit with a muddler, then place the crushed fruit in a fine-mesh wire sieve. Use your muddler to force the purée through the sieve, mashing until all liquid has been extracted from the pulp (discard the remaining trapped seeds and solids). One pear yields around 1 ounce of purée.

Created in 2008 by Brother Cleve, the Boston-based mixologist and musician who kick-started the 1990s "Cocktail Nation" scene with the neo-lounge band Combustible Edison. "This drink is my homage to Donn Beach," says Cleve. "The way he combined so many flavors to make one perfect drink is awe-inspiring. When I first tasted the prickly pear 'cactus juice,' I wanted to try to approach it like Donn would." And the name? "I've watched cactus flowers bloom and dug

New Orleans bartender Chris Hannah's Tiki-inspired drinks are turning Arnaud's restaurant bar, the French 75, into the French Polynesian 75. Chris's secret weapon is the syrups he makes at home, then brings to work to put in his cocktails. We're especially fond of his coffee syrup, which can stand on its own as an after-dinner dram. (Or try it in a Kiliki Cooler, page 181.)

COLIBRI

1 ½ ounces chocolate & vanilla rum
  infusion*
1 ½ ounces Colibri pre-mix**
Demerara sugar
Coconut flakes, toasted

Step one: **Mix the demerara sugar and toasted coconut flakes in a dish. Wet the outside rim of a cocktail glass with a little lime juice and roll it in** the sugar-coconut mix. Chill the glass. **Step two: In your cocktail shaker, combine the rum infusion and pre-mix. Add ice and shake the hell out of it. Strain into the chilled glass and serve.**

*CHOCOLATE & VANILLA-INFUSED RUM: Coarsely chop 1 ½ ounces of high-quality unsweetened chocolate, then put it in a full 750 ml bottle of mellow amber rum, such as Angostura 1919 or Mount Gay. Seal it and let sit for 3 days, swirling it occasionally. When the three days are up, strain out the chocolate by pouring the infused rum through a coffee filter into a clean bottle. Put half of a vanilla bean in the bottle, and cap it. Your infusion is now ready to use.

**COLIBRI PRE-MIX: Combine 8 ounces sweetened condensed milk (use a brand whose ingredients are milk and sugar and nothing else, such as Eagle or Magnolia) and 16 ounces unsweetened coconut water (available canned in gourmet markets). Shake well and refrigerate. (Should keep for 2 to 3 days; shake again before using.)

Created in 2005 for the Manhattan restaurant 5 Ninth by David Wondrich, drinks columnist for Esquire *magazine, wine and spirits editor of* Saveur *magazine, and author of several cocktail books (including the James Beard Award-winning* Imbibe! *and the upcoming* Punch, or the Delights and Dangers of the Flowing Bowl). "The Colibri is named after the Taino indian word for 'hummingbird,'" says David, who warns that the drink "will turn you into a hovering nectar-sipper before you can say 'hovering nectar-sipper.' It's based on a 19th-cen-*

tury recipe in Terrington's Cooling Cups and Dainty Drinks, *although I added the coconut water and condensed milk."*

CUZCO FIZZ

5 green grapes
¾ ounce fresh lime juice
2 ounces pisco
1 oz. St-Germain elderflower liqueur
½ ounce club soda

Muddle the grapes in your cocktail shaker. Add pisco, lime juice, St-Germain, and ice cubes. Shake and strain into an old-fashioned glass filled with fresh ice. Top with club soda.

Lynette Marrero created this in 2007, while tending bar at Freeman's restaurant on Manhattan's Lower East Side. She now runs a cocktail consulting company called Drinks At Six. (Six? Who waits till six?)

Max's Mistake (left), Dead Reckoning (center),
Xtabay (right) | Martin Cate

1 ounce fresh lemon juice
1 ounce unsweetened pineapple juice
½ ounce Navan vanilla liqueur
½ ounce tawny Port
½ ounce maple syrup (grade A only)
2 ounces Cockspur 12-year V.S.O.R. rum (or sub Mount Gay 12-year Extra Old)
1 ounce soda water
Dash Angostura bitters

Shake everything – except soda – with ice. Stir in soda. Strain into a tall glass filled with fresh ice. Garnish with a pineapple wedge, a mint sprig, and a length of spiral-cut lemon peel (pictured opposite).

"I fell in love with tiki," says Martin Cate, "at a 1994 visit to Trader Vic's in Washington, D.C." So much so that he eventually got himself a job tending bar at the San Francisco Vic's. After apprenticing there for a year, in 2006 he opened the Forbidden Island Tiki Lounge across the bay in Alameda, for which he hand-picked 106 rums, hand-made his own liqueurs and syrups, and mixed them in his own recipes – such as the Dead Reckoning, a 2007 creation which the San Francisco Chronicle *called "a dreamy cool breeze of a drink, fruity but not too sweet with elusive flavors that beckon you deeper and deeper into the glass." Martin has since set sail from Forbidden Island and is now the owner of Smuggler's Cove, a new bar in San Francisco "dedicated to the world of rum and exotic cocktails."*

6 ounces Wray & Nephew Overproof White rum
Zest of 9 medium limes, with no traces of white pith
40 whole cloves
1 ½ ounces (by weight) peeled, julienned fresh ginger
2 tablespoons blanched, slivered almonds (dry toasted until golden brown)
14 ounces cold process 2:1 simple syrup*
¼ teaspoon almond extract
4 ½ ounces fresh lime juice, strained

Step one: **Combine the rum, lime zest, cloves and ginger in a jar and seal, letting the mixture soak for 24 hours. Then strain through moistened cheesecloth, squeezing the solids to extract all liquid.** *Step two:* **Add the almond extract, sugar syrup and lime juice. Shake it all together and serve. It'll keep in the fridge for about a month.**

*COLD-PROCESS 2:1 SYRUP: two parts superfine sugar to one part warm water, shaken in a jar until all the sugar is dissolved. (We are told that not using heat results in a crisper syrup with a lighter density, one that plays better with falernum's flavors than a cooked syrup.)

You've probably noticed by now that falernum pops up in a lot of exotic drink recipes. The aromatic ginger-lime syrup is commercially available (see page 225), but more adventurous gastronauts might want to try making their own. That's what Paul Clarke did when he couldn't find falernum in his home town – a

big problem when your job is writing about cocktails for the San Francisco Chronicle, Imbibe *magazine*, and the drink blog cocktailchronicles.com. It took Paul over a year of experimentation to come up with his Falernum #9; he would have gone to #10, but the pragmatist in him won out over the perfectionist. "You have no idea how my family was reacting to a refrigerator full of mason jars with green, funky-smelling liquids in them," says Paul. "And that's in the spaces between the vermouth bottles."

FAREWELL FLIP

35 ml (just over 1 ounce) El Dorado 12-year Demerara rum
15 ml (½ ounce) Carpano Antica vermouth
15 ml (½ ounce) heavy cream
10 ml (1/3 ounce) Cherry Heering
2.5 ml (¾ teaspoon) sugar syrup
2.5 ml (¾ teaspoon) vanilla extract
1 egg yolk

Shake like hell with plenty of ice cubes. Strain into an old-fashioned glass. Dust with grated nutmeg and cherry-chocolate flakes.

By Ladislav Piljar, bar manager at Mark's Bar, Hix Restaurant, London, England.

Ladislav tended bar in Slovakia, France, and Ireland before moving to London, an occasion he marked with this 2009 drink. He blogs at classicbartending.com.

GANTT'S TOMB

¾ ounce fresh pineapple juice (see Beach Bum on page 192)
½ ounce fresh lemon juice
½ ounce orange juice
½ ounce sugar syrup
1 ounce Gosling's Black Seal rum
1 ounce Rittenhouse 100-proof rye (can sub Wild Turkey 101-proof rye)
½ ounce El Dorado 151-proof rum
¼ ounce pimento liqueur (see page 230)

Shake with three ice cubes and strain into a pilsner glass filled with crushed ice. Garnish with a mint sprig.

By Brian Miller, head bartender at Death & Company, Manhattan, 2008. "This was my first stab at creating a new Tiki drink," Brian told the Bum. "I was inspired by the Zombie and tried to create something with many layers to it. I also wanted to try and appeal to the cocktail geeks of the world who are so critical of Tiki drinks. Most consider them syrupy, sweet concoctions that have no place in the true cocktail pantheon. So I decided to do some-

Garrett's Maitini | Brian Powers

thing with a mix of rum and Rittenhouse rye — a favorite spirit amongst the geeks. And of course I named it after Donn," whose real name was Ernest Raymond Beaumont Gantt. "He's the one I would most like to emulate," adds Brian, "not only in the Tiki world but the entire cocktail world as well."

GARRETT'S MAITINI

1 ½ ounces Bacardi 8 rum
½ ounce orgeat syrup
½ ounce orange Curacao
½ ounce fresh kalamansi lime juice*
    (reserve shells)
½ ounce fresh orange juice
Dark Jamaican rum (float)

Shake everything — except dark Jamaican rum — with ice. Strain into a chilled cocktail glass. Float three of your spent kalamansi shells on top of the drink, then fill each with dark Jamaican rum (as in the photo above). Garnish with a strip of orange peel.

*KALAMANSI LIME: A tiny Southeast Asian fruit that tastes like a cross between lime and tangerine. You can substitute key limes, which are roughly the same size.

In August of 2009, the Bum was invited to judge a Mai Tai competition at the Royal Kona Resort in Hawaii. The 29 contest finalists, most of them locals, ingeniously applied techniques from the front lines of today's cocktail renaissance to their Mai Tai variations: some went molecular with orgeat foam, hickory smoke infusion, and flamed orange mist, while others followed the farm-to-glass dictum with locally sourced dragon fruit and home-made coconut bitters. Royal Kona bartender Garrett Gresham won the "People's Choice" award with his Maitini.

ALOHA IO HALAU
(WELCOME TO THIS HOUSE.)

GINGER & LYCHEE CAIPIRISSIMA

2 fresh lychee nuts, shelled
Half of a lime, cut into quarters
½ ounce sugar syrup
½ ounce ginger syrup (see page 226)
¼ teaspoon falernum
2 ounces Bacardi Añejo rum

Place lime quarters, lychee nuts, syrups and falernum in your cocktail shaker. Muddle thoroughly, extracting the juice from the lime and the oil from the peel. Add rum. Shake well with ice cubes. Pour entire contents unstrained into a chilled old-fashioned glass.

The dean of American bartenders — who have nicknamed him "King Cocktail" — Dale DeGroff is the founding President of the Museum Of The American Cocktail, and author of the books The Essential Cocktail *and* The Craft Of The Cocktail. *The King is widely credited with bringing mixed drinks out of the dark ages of the*

1980s (when wine spritzers and chemical Margarita mix ruled the day) with new twists on classic recipes, made with fresh ingredients. He's also well-versed in Tiki, having in 2005 revamped the drink menu at the Halekulani on Waikiki Beach — for which he created the Caipirissima.

GLASS BOTTOM BOAT

Half of a fresh lemon, cut into wedges with pits removed
A ring of fresh-cut pineapple, broken into wedges
2 brandied cherries*
2 teaspoons brown sugar
2 ounces Goslings Black Seal rum
2 ounces Belgian apple lambic beer (such as Lindemans Pomme)

In a cocktail shaker, thoroughly muddle cherries, pineapple, lemon and sugar. Add rum, fill with ice, and shake. Pour entire contents into a double old fashioned glass, Caipirinha-style, and top with apple lambic beer. Stir to combine. Garnish with a paper parasol stuck to a pineapple wedge and cherry.

*BRANDIED CHERRIES: A more natural alternative to maraschino cocktail cherries. If you can't find them, this drink also works well with canned tart cherries packed in water (cheap and always in stock in your local supermarket).

By Sonya Runkle. Now based in Minneapolis, Sonya was a San Francisco bartender who won several cocktail competitions before creating this drink in 2006. Her inspiration? According to wit-

nesses, she threw it together on the spot by muddling whatever was in the garnish tray in front of her. The name refers not to the famous Catalina Island tourist attraction, but to a sexual fetish involving two consenting adults and a glass coffee table. (Don't look it up until after you've finished your drink.)

HONOLULU HONEY

20ml (2/3 ounce) fresh lime juice
20ml (2/3 ounce) mango puree*
20ml (2/3 ounce) Jules' honey cream**
40ml (1 1/3 ounces) unsweetened
    pineapple juice
50ml (1 2/3 ounces) gold puerto Rican
    rum

Place everything in a blender without ice. Blend at high speed for at least one full minute, until the honey cream has thoroughly integrated with the other ingredients, turning the drink an opaque pumpkin color. Pour into a cocktail shaker filled with ice cubes. Shake long and hard, then strain into a wahine mug filled with fresh ice. Garnish with a hibiscus flower.

*MANGO PUREE: Mahiki uses the Funkin brand, but if there are Latino markets in your town look for frozen packets under the Goya, El Sembrador, or La Fé labels.

**JULES' HONEY CREAM: Equal parts brown sugar, unsalted butter, and honey, heated under a low flame until thoroughly liquefied and combined. Don't make more than you plan to use at one time, as refrigeration will harden it beyond usability.

A throwback to the glamorous beginnings of Tiki, when Marlene Dietrich frequented Don The Beachcomber's and Queen Elizabeth dined at Trader Vic's, the Mahiki nightclub is catnip for London's paparazzi: Madonna, Paris Hilton, and the Royal Family are regulars (Prince Harry reportedly ran up a £22,000 tab in one night). But proprietor "Papa Jules" Gualdoni is the perfect host whether you're a prince or a pauper. The Honolulu Honey, created in 2006 by Michael Butt of the UK cocktail consortium The Soul Shakers, employs Jules' recipe for honey cream, which Jules cooks nightly behind the bar.

INCLEMENT WEATHER

1 ounce Powers Irish whiskey
1 ounce Mandarin Napoleon liqueur
    (or sub Grand Marnier)
2 barspoons honey
1 lemon
1 orange

Step one: Top and tail the lemon and orange, then cut several small tri-

angle-shaped pieces from each. Place lemon triangles in an old-fashioned glass until the glass is one-quarter full, then fill the glass to the halfway point with orange triangles. Muddle the fruit in the glass, and set glass aside. *Step two:* In a separate vessel, dissolve the honey in the whiskey. Then pour the honeyed whiskey over the muddled fruit, add Mandarin liqueur and crushed ice to fill, and churn it all up until well-chilled. Garnish with orange and lemon wheels, and serve with 2 short straws.

In the heart of Amsterdam, just off Rembrandt Square, the tiny speakeasy Door 74 is cross-breeding a new strain of offbeat exotics — such as this 2008 "Irish Caipirinha" by proprietor Philip Duff. "'Oranges and lemons, say the bells of St. Clements' is a popular playground rhyme in Ireland," explains Philip, a cocktail consultant who trained over 6,000 bartenders in 30 countries before roosting in Holland to open his own bar. "This drink marries those familiar flavors with the decidedly cold-weather Irish whiskey, honeyed and fruity."

KIWI'S NEST GROG

1 whole fresh lemon, cut into quarters
Half of a fresh Kiwi fruit, skin removed
1 ounce amber Martinique rum
1 ounce light Virgin Islands rum
½ ounce dark Jamaican rum
1 ounce orgeat syrup
¼ ounce pimento liqueur (see page 230)
Dash orange bitters

In a cocktail shaker, thoroughly muddle kiwi and lemon to extract all juice. Add all other ingredients and shake well with ice cubes. Strain into a tall glass filled with crushed ice. Garnish with a kiwi fruit wheel.

By Cass McClure, a ceramicist whose company, Ocea Otica, specializes in hand-crafted Tiki mugs and bowls (see page 12). He also specializes in what to put in them, such as this 2008 concoction. "Kiwi fruit can always be found in our fridge, as it is a staple of my iguana's diet," says Cass. "It commonly has found its way into cocktails at home for years." The kiwi fruit, that is — not the iguana.

KON TIKI TI-PUNCH

20 ml (2/3 ounce) fresh lime juice
15 ml (½ ounce) grenadine
50 ml (1 2/3 ounces) Bacardi 8 rum
Teaspoon demerara sugar syrup (see page 225)
Teaspoon guava jelly
A chunk of fresh pineapple

In your cocktail shaker, thoroughly muddle the pineapple chunk and guava jelly in lime juice. Add rum, grenadine, and demerara syrup. Shake with ice and strain into a punch goblet filled with a large ice cube (pictured opposite). Garnish with a lime wedge, pineapple chunk and a mint sprig tip.

Northern Ireland is the last place we expected to find an authentic, meticulously prepared 1934 Don The Beachcomber Zombie or 1944 Trader Vic Mai Tai. But find them we did, at the bar of the Merchant Hotel in Belfast. Under the stewardship of "Bar & Potation Manager"

Kon Tiki Ti-Punch | Merchant Hotel/Lisa Anne McCarron

Sean Muldoon, the Merchant takes Tiki so seriously that it tracked down an extremely rare vintage bottle of 17-year Wray & Nephew rum — the rum with which Trader Vic originally mixed his Mai Tais — so that patrons can experience the drink as it was meant to be. (Before you order one, you might want to catch yourself a leprechaun: given the value of that bottle, one Mai Tai will cost you around $1,000.) The Merchant also offers contemporary exotic drinks created by Sean, such as his 2007 Kon Tiki Ti-Punch.

LITTLE POLYNESIAN

25 ml (5/6 ounce) fresh lime juice
20 ml (2/3 ounce) Appleton V/X rum
20 ml (2/3 ounce) dark Jamaican rum
10 ml (1/3 ounce) orange Curacao
10 ml (1/3 ounce) demerara sugar
    syrup (see page 225)
2 fresh kumquats, cut into quarters

In your cocktail shaker, thoroughly muddle kumquat quarters in lime juice. Add rums, Curacao, and demerara syrup. Shake with ice and strain into an old-fashioned glass filled with fresh ice. Garnish with a lime wheel and two kumquat discs.

Created in 2007 by Sean Muldoon of the Merchant Hotel bar, Belfast, Ireland (see Kon Tiki Ti-Punch above).

MAX'S MISTAKE

1 ounce fresh lemon juice
1 ounce passion fruit syrup
½ oz honey mix (see page 226)
2 ounces Plymouth gin
2 ounces Lorina Sparkling Lemonade
    (or any quality sparkling lemonade)
Dash Angostura bitters
1 cup (8 ounces) half-sized ice cubes
    (chipped ice)

Put everything in a blender. Pulse blend for about 2-3 seconds. Pour entire contents into a goblet (pictured page 196, on left). If necessary, add more ice to fill.

Martin Cate (see Dead Reckoning above) created this drink in 2005, when he was tending bar at Trader Vic's in San Francisco. Most blended tropicals call for crushed ice, but Martin has made a study of the blender and recommends what he calls "half-cube chip ice," the kind you buy in bags at the supermarket as opposed to the larger cubes you make at home in the freezer (which you can crack into smaller pieces as well). "Crushed ice in a drink mixer — while frosting the glass nicely — dilutes a little too fast," says Mar-

Mexican Headhunter | Rikki Brodrick

tin. "I think half-cube works perfectly. Some of it gets broken up, so you get mixed-texture ice and a good froth, especially when you blend with a carbonated ingredient."

MEXICAN HEADHUNTER

30 ml (1 ounce) Arette Reposado tequila
20 ml (2/3 ounce) Arette Añejo tequila
20 ml (2/3 ounce) fresh lemon juice
15 ml (½ ounce) sage gomme*
15 ml (½ ounce) honey mix (see page 226)
5 ml (just under a teaspoon) ginger juice
40 ml (1 1/3 ounces) unsweetened pineapple juice
2 dashes orange bitters

Shake with ice cubes. Strain into a Trailer Happiness headhunter mug

(pictured above) filled with fresh ice.

*SAGE GOMME: A sage-infused, cold-process sugar syrup. Add 1 cup sugar to 1 cup cold water, shake or stir till sugar dissolves, then add 5 fresh sage leaves. Cover and let steep for 24 to 36 hours, or until you have a pleasant sage taste.

A 2009 concoction by Rikki Brodrick, general manager of Trailer Happiness, London, England. Just as Donn Beach mixed different rums in one drink to goose the base flavor, Rikki here blends reposado and añejo tequilas. In fact, he says, the Mexican Headhunter was directly inspired by Donn: "Having loved the Zombie so much, we just felt that there must be a way to get a similar effect with our second favourite spirit. So the tequila Zombie was born!" Donn's love of showmanship also informs the Headhunter mug, conceived "after a few drinks one night" and crafted by British

Created in 2008 by Jim Meehan, deputy editor of Food & Wine Cocktails, *co-editor of* Mr. Boston Official Bartender's Guide, *and general manager of PDT in Manhattan. Having mastered classic cocktail construction while tending bar at Gramercy Tavern, the Pegu Club, and PDT, Jim is no longer content merely balancing elements of sweet and sour, floral and spice in his original drinks. "My new interest," he says, "is incorporating smoke." Most mixologists turn to Scotch for smokiness, but Jim's taste for the exotic led him to mezcal.*

mug-maker Jamie "Cheeky Tiki" Wilson. The hat brim does double-duty as straw holder and nachos plate, for streamlined sippin' and chippin'.

OPAKA RAKA

1 ½ ounces Junipero gin*
1 ½ ounces Donn's spices #2**
¾ ounce fresh lime juice
¼ ounce simple syrup
1 dash Elemakule Tiki bitters (sub Fee's Whiskey Barrel Aged bitters)

Shake everything with ice cubes. Strain into a tall glass filled with fresh ice. Garnish with a lime wheel.

*JUNIPERO: This small-batch gin has a proof of 98.6, the same number as normal human body temperature. Don't substitute a gin with less than 94-proof, or the Opaka will lose its snap (we got good results with Tanqueray).

MEZCAL MULE

¾ ounce fresh lime juice
¾ ounce passion fruit purée
1 ounce ginger beer
3 slices fresh cucumber, skin removed
1 ½ ounces mezcal (Sombra preferred)
Ground chili

Muddle the cucumber in your cocktail shaker. Add passion fruit purée, lime juice, mezcal, ginger beer, and ice cubes. Shake, then strain into an old-fashioned glass filled with fresh ice. Sprinkle a pinch of ground chili, and garnish with a piece of candied ginger speared to a slice of cucumber.

**DONN'S SPICES #2: Decoded by the Bum in his book *Sippin' Safari*, this is Don The Beachcomber's secret 1937 blend of equal parts vanilla syrup and pimento liqueur.

By Brian Miller of Death & Company in Manhattan (see Gantt's Tomb on page

198), 2007. *"This is my answer to the Donga Punch in Sippin' Safari,"* says Brian. *"After making Donn's Spices #2, I fell in love with the flavor profile and wanted to do something with it and gin, and the Bittermens Elemakule bitters that my good friend Avery named after me — 'elemakule' meaning 'old man' in Hawaiian. That's what all these young and much more talented bartenders call me. If only I knew then what I know now."*

ORGEAT PUNCH

½ ounce fresh lime juice
½ ounce fresh lemon juice
½ ounce limoncello
1 ounce orgeat syrup
1 ½ ounces spiced rum
½ ounce 151-proof Caribbean rum
(Cruzan or Bacardi)

Shake well with crushed ice. Pour unstrained into a tall glass.

Lu Brow, the head mixologist at Cafe Adelaide's Swizzle Stick Bar in New Orleans, says that this is her version of the Roosevelt Hotel's 1860s Orgeat Punch. She is too modest. Her punch bears scant resemblance to the original, which called for rye and Port wine.

ORGEAT SYRUP

500 grams (17 ½ ounces) blanched
almonds
800 ml (27 ounces) water
700 grams (a little over 1 ½ pounds)
table sugar
100 ml (3 1/3 ounces) vodka or brandy
2 tablespoons orange flower water or
rose flower water (optional)

Step one: Place the almonds in a bowl, cover bowl with cold water, and let almonds soak for 30 minutes. Drain and discard the water, then crush the almonds with a rolling pin (or you can chop them to a fine grind in a food processor). *Step two:* Transfer the crushed almonds to a large bowl and mix them with the 800 ml water. Let stand for one to two hours. *Step three:* Into another bowl of equal size, strain the almond and water mixture through a layer of cheesecloth, squeezing the cloth to extract all liquid. Put the chopped almonds back into this strained almond water, let stand for another hour, and then strain again. Repeat a third time if you wish. (This is will get all the oils out of the almonds.) *Step four:* Pour the strained liquid into a pan, discarding the almond pulp. Add the sugar to the pan and cook over a gentle heat, stirring constantly. Remove from heat when the sugar is completely dissolved. Let cool for 15 minutes, then add the orange flower water and the brandy or vodka. Store your orgeat in a clean glass bottle. (This recipe yields about 1 ½ liters, or 50 ounces).

In their thirst for the artisanal, today's hardcore cocktailians find commercially processed orgeat syrups wanting. In 2006, Canadian mixologist Darcy O'Neil decided to take a stand against artificial ingredients and create his own orgeat. He's uniquely qualified to do so: Darcy is not only a professional bartender, he's a professional chemist. When not working behind the mahogany at Braise restaurant in London, Ontario, Darcy writes about the relationship between hard science and hard liquor on his blog artofdrink.com.

Pimento liqueur

PAMPLEMOUSSE PUNCH

2 ounces white grapefruit juice
1 ounce spiced rum
1 ounce Clément Creole Shrubb*
Dash Angostura bitters
6 drops (1/8 teaspoon) Herbsaint or
   Pernod

Shake well with ice cubes. Pour unstrained into an old-fashioned glass. Garnish with lengths of spiral-cut grapefruit and orange peel, coiled inside the glass.

*CREOLE SHRUBB: A Curacao-type orange liqueur made with Clément rum and West Indian spices. More assertive and less sweet than normal Curacao.

By Wayne Curtis, drinks columnist for The Atlantic *magazine and author of the book* And A Bottle Of Rum: A History Of The New World In Ten Cocktails. *Wayne created the Pamplemousse Punch for a 2008 Tiki-themed dinner he co-hosted with the Bum at the Country Club in New Orleans. Along with chef Chris DeBarr's flaming Tiki-shaped*

Baked Alaska, this drink was the hit of the evening.

PIMENTO LIQUEUR

¼ cup dried whole allspice berries
1 fifth-sized bottle (750 ml) light Virgin
   Islands rum
2 cups (1 pound) brown sugar
1 cup water

Step one: **Grind the allspice berries until they have the consistency of ground coffee. Place your ground allspice in a saucepan with 1 cup of light rum and bring to a boil, then turn off the heat and stir. This will make a tea. Funnel this hot tea, ground berries and all, into an empty rum bottle. Now fill the bottle ¾ of the way to the top with more of the same light rum. Seal it and let sit for at least 2 weeks, shaking it daily.** Step two: **When the 2 weeks are up, filter through a double-layer of cheesecloth. Discard solids, then filter again through a metal mesh coffee filter, and a third time through unbleached paper filters. (If the resulting reddish brown liquid is still cloudy, filter once more through the paper.)**

Now make a sugar syrup by heating 1 cup water and 1 pound brown sugar until the sugar is dissolved. Mix equal parts of this sugar syrup with your pimento-infused rum. Step three: Bottle it, seal it, and let it sit unmolested for at least a month. (The longer you wait, the more flavorful it gets.)

There's a growing subset of drink-fanciers called "distologists," who craft their own liquors and liqueurs at home. Among Tiki-philes, Matthew "Kuku Ahu" Thatcher is the go-to distologist. We went to him when we could no longer find pimento liqueur on U.S. shelves, and he hipped us to this surprisingly simple recipe, which he created in 2005. "I just like to tinker with booze and study it a little," says Kuku, who hangs his hat in Columbus, Ohio. "That's really where it begins and ends with me. I do it for myself and for the drinkers."

POLOLU

2 ounces gin
1 ounce Cognac
1 ounce unsweetened pineapple juice
½ ounce orange Curacao
½ ounce St-Germain elderflower
    liqueur
½ ounce Lopez coconut cream
2 dashes orange bitters
Ground cinnamon

Shake everything – except cinnamon – with plenty of ice cubes. Strain into a cocktail glass. Top with a generous pinch of cinnamon, and garnish with a pineapple leaf.

Under his nom de Tiki Dr. Bamboo, Craig Mrusek writes the drinks column for Bachelor Pad magazine and the cocktail

blog drbambooblogspot.com. "I was intrigued by the idea of coming up with a Tiki-style drink that didn't use rum," he says of the Polulu. "So I made gin the base and used the Painkiller (one of my favorites) as inspiration. It's also got some of the same DNA as the Fogcutter, so I figure that's a pretty good pedigree."

PUNKY MONKEY

1 ounce Scarlet Ibis rum*
1 ounce 90-proof bourbon (Buffalo
    Trace preferred)
½ ounce sugar syrup
½ ounce fresh lemon juice
½ ounce fresh pineapple juice (see
    Beach Bum, page 192)
Dash Angostura bitters
Dash Peychaud's bitters
5 green cardamom pods

Lightly muddle the cardamom pods. Add all other ingredients, then shake well with ice cubes. Strain through a fine-mesh wire sieve into a champagne coupe.

*SCARLET IBIS: Death & Company had this 98-proof blend of Trinidad rums specially tailored for them, so that they could craft cocktails like this one. There's no real substitute for it (that's why they had to have it made); the closest pinch-hitters we can think of are Sea Wynde or Santa Teresa 1796.

Created in 2008 by Joaquin Simo, who tends bar at Death & Company in Manhattan. This drink is on the menu there as the Kerala, because management wouldn't let Joaquin call it Punky Monkey. In the name of monkeys everywhere, we have here corrected that injustice.

REVERB CRASH

¾ ounce fresh lime juice
4 ounces grapefruit Juice
1 ½ ounces passion fruit syrup
3 teaspoons orgeat syrup
1 ¼ ounces light Virgin Islands rum
1 ¼ ounces dark Jamaican rum

Shake everything with ice cubes. Pour unstrained into a tall glass or Tiki mug (pictured opposite). Garnish with a mint sprig.

The online chat room Tiki Central is the place to go for intel on all tropics topics. Of particular interest to imbibers is the site's "Tiki Drinks and Food" forum. That's where we found this recipe by San Diego musician Ran Mosessco, who won the 2003 Tiki Central Drink Contest with it. Ran originally hails from Israel, where he co-founded a surf band called The Astroglides; their repertoire includes "Cruisin' Down Menahem Begin Boulevard" and "The Adventures Of Rabbi Jacob." L'chaim, dude!

RUMSCULLION

2 ounces aged Demerara rum (El Dorado 12-year preferred)
1 ounce Punt e Mes*
Teaspoon falernum
8 drops Herbsaint
Dash Fee's Old Fashion bitters (can sub Angostura)

Stir with cracked ice until well chilled. Strain into a chilled cocktail glass. Garnish with a long orange twist, expressing the oil from the peel into the drink.

*PUNT E MES: A brand of Italian vermouth infused with herbs and citrus. Great stuff, but hard to find. Substitute a top-shelf Italian vermouth, such as Carpano Antica or Vya (if you can't find those either, the drink still works with good old Martini & Rossi red).

Created in 2008 by Craig Hermann, who's currently behind the stick at Thatch Tiki Bar in Portland, Oregon. Craig also writes about tropical drinks on his blog, coloneltiki.com. Says he: "This drink came from a recent series of experiments whose goal was to create a cocktail that might have existed if the Polynesian Pop movement cohabited, anachronistically, during Prohibition."

SAGE BON VIVANT

2 sage leaves
2 small chunks of fresh pineapple
10 ml (1/3 ounce) sugar syrup
20 ml (2/3 ounce) fresh lime juice
25 ml (5/6 ounce) home-made sage liqueur*
50 ml (1 2/3 ounces) Havana Club 5-year Cuban rum**

In your cocktail shaker, muddle the sage leaves, pineapple chunks, and sugar syrup. Add the lime juice, rum, sage liqueur and ice. Shake. Strain through a fine-mesh wire sieve into a cocktail glass. Garnish with a sage leaf floating on top of drink.

*SAGE LIQUEUR: Add 30 grams (just a hair over 1 ounce) fresh sage leaves to a full 750 ml bottle of 100-proof Smirnoff vodka or an overproof medium-bodied rum. Let sit in a dark place, at room temperature, for eight days.

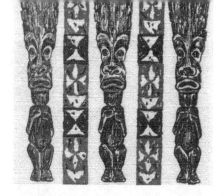

Shake well with plenty of ice cubes. Strain into an old-fashioned glass. Garnish with an orchid.

*SOURSOP NECTAR: Also known as guanabana nectar. Look for the Foco brand in Asian markets; JIC also makes a mixable nectar. Avoid Jumex and Goya.

Created by Audrey "Libation Goddess" Saunders in 2004, when she was Beverage Director of Bemelmans Bar in Manhattan. A year later Audrey opened her own bar, the Pegu Club, which serves impeccable classic cocktails and wildly imaginative originals amid elegant decor that references Burma under the British Raj.

Then strain out the solids and mix the liquid infusion with 250 grams (a little over 1 cup) of a 3:2 sugar syrup (that's 3 parts sugar to 2 parts water, heated until sugar dissolves, then cooled to room temperature).

**CUBAN RUM: As of this writing, still unavailable in the U.S. Substitute Flor De Caña 5-year Black Label or 7-year Grand Reserve.

Created in 2008 by Stanislav Vadrna, globe-trotting spirits educator based in Bratislava, Slovakia. Want to know the best way to position your feet when shaking a cocktail? Ask Stan. Curious about the 'Ichigo-Ichie' Japanese bartending philosophy? Ask Stan. Need an exotic cocktail recipe using ingredients you've never seen in a drink before? Ask Stan. We did, and he answered with the Sage Bon Vivant. He calls it, tongue not entirely in cheek, "the best-ever short tropical aphrodisiac drink."

SOURSOP SOUR

¾ ounce fresh lemon juice
1 ounce sugar syrup
3 ounces Foco soursop nectar*
1 ½ ounces gin
2 dashes Angostura bitters

STEPHEN REMSBERG'S PLANTER'S PUNCH

Juice of half a large lime (around ¾ ounce)
1 ounce sugar syrup
3 ounces Coruba dark Jamaican rum
3 dashes Angostura bitters

Place all of the above in a large tall glass (preferably a 14-ounce Zombie glass). Fill glass with crushed ice and swizzle vigorously until well-chilled. After swizzling the ice will settle, so add more to fill. Garnish with a mint sprig. "I am not offended by an orange slice and a cocktail cherry," allows Stephen.

Stephen Remsberg owns the world's largest private rum collection. In addition to rarities from New England and Egypt, some bottled over 100 years ago, his New Orleans home warehouses rums from Uganda and Nepal; there's even one from

Korea with a snake inside the bottle. Stephen's predilection for Jamaica's rums eventually led him to Jamaica's national drink. "I've played with the Planter's Punch for 20 years," he told the Bum. "Ten or 12 years ago I became satisfied that I'd found nirvana, and stopped experimenting."

STORM CLOUD RISING

1 ½ ounces Mount Gay Extra Old 12-year rum (or Cockspur 12-year V.S.O.R.)
½ ounce Domaine de Canton ginger liqueur
6 ounces ice-cold ginger beer
Small scoop of vanilla bean ice cream

Stir together rum, liqueur, and ginger beer in a tulip glass. Add ice cream, then stir until mixture foams up to fill glass (creating your "storm cloud rising"). Garnish with a lime wheel.

By Blair Reynolds, 2008. Blair's a bartender based in Portland, Oregon, where he presides over "Tiki Tuesdays" at the Teardrop Lounge. He also blogs about tropical drinks on tradertiki.com.

THAITI HAMOA

½ ounce fresh lime juice
2 ounces banana flambé mix*
3 ounces black Assam tea, chilled
1 ½ ounces Pyrat XO Rum (or sub gold Jamaican)

Place everything in a cocktail shaker with a cup of ice. Roll back and forth several times until chilled, then pour unstrained into a double old-fashioned glass. Garnish with a sprig of mint and an orange twist.

*BANANA FLAMBÉ MIX: In a large saucepan over medium heat, melt 1 tablespoon dark muscovado sugar until it starts to caramelize. Add 2 teaspoons butter, 1 ounce each orange and lime juices, and 1 peeled and diced banana. Cook for 1 minute, stirring constantly until most of the liquid is evaporated. Remove pan from heat and add 2 ounces Navan vanilla liqueur. Put pan back on the heat; it should flambé. Continue to cook for about 1 minute, then add a sprinkle of garam masala spice mix (available at grocery stores on the spice rack). Pour this mixture unstrained into a bowl and refrigerate. Yields four servings.

Before becoming Chairman of the U.S. Bartenders Guild Nevada Chapter, Francesco Lafranconi won more international cocktail competitions than you can shake a swizzle stick at. In fact, he's only made one false move in his entire career — and that's inviting the Beachbum to co-host a "Tiki Beach" presentation at the 2008 Tampa Wine & Food festival, for which Francesco created the Thaiti Hamoa. The Bum was charged with mixing a sample batch for the audience; unacquainted with that level of exertion, he neglected to add the flambé mix to the samples. For some reason Francesco is still talking to us. Here's what he says about the Thaiti Hamoa: "I developed it by combining some old-school tableside flambé dessert techniques with an exotic rum drink. It's a great batched long drink to serve in pitchers at Tiki parties, or whenever great cocktails deserve to be shared among friends and family."

THE MAI TAI 3000

1 "lime chip" (Freeze one lime. Slice thinly in a deli slicer. Soak slices in sugar syrup, place on a tray, and place tray in oven at 100° Fahrenheit until sugar has slightly caramelized. Let cool.)

1 "rum square" (Place 3 ounces water and 1 teaspoon agar in a pot for 15 minutes, heating until all agar is dissolved. Add 3 ounces Appleton V/X rum and 1 ounce Lemon Hart 151 rum, and stir well. Pour carefully into a shallow tray and refrigerate. Cut into squares when solid.)

1 dollop "orgeat foam" (Place 4 ounces orgeat syrup, 2 ounces water, 2 dashes Angostura bitters, and 3 egg whites into an iSi Cream Whipper Charger and charge.)

1 fine pinch of orange zest (freshly grated orange peel)

Place the rum square on top of the lime chip, then top the rum square with foam. Finish off with a pinch of orange zest (see opposite photo for reference). To "drink," place all in mouth at once and chew.

By Jamie Boudreau, 2008. The Seattle Times called Jamie "The Cocktail Whisperer" for the way he gives new life to old drinks using the techniques of molecular mixology. (Inspired by the gastronomy-as-chemistry experiments of Spain's El Bulli restaurant in the 1990s, molecular mixology is a kind of postmodern drink deconstruction.) Jamie took time out from running Seattle's Tini Bigs bar to explain how he went molecular on the Mai Tai: "Trader Vic's original recipe called for rum, lime, orange Curacao, rock candy and orgeat. When building the Mai Tai 3000, I had to keep these flavors in mind for the 'drink' to be recognizable, but at the same time I wanted to add new textures. So I replaced the rock candy with the simple syrup that soaked the lime chips, and the Curacao with a touch of orange zest on top of the foam. The orgeat in foam form allows the powerful flavor of almond to be softened by the 'airiness' of the egg white foam." Jamie crafted this Jetsonian amuse-bouche to "get the customer's taste buds tingling, perhaps in anticipation of a 'real' Mai Tai next."*

VAVA VOOM

25 ml (5/6 ounce) fresh lime juice
10 ml (1/3 ounce) white crème de cacao
10 ml (1/3 ounce) apricot brandy
60 ml (2 ounces) Brugal Añejo rum (or sub gold Puerto Rican)
7.5 ml (¼ ounce) sugar syrup
Generous dash Angostura bitters
Generous dash Fee's Old Fashion bitters

Shake with ice cubes and strain into a chilled 5-ounce cocktail coupette. Garnish with a lime wedge.

"It's a simple twist on the Pegu Club cocktail," says Belfast bartender Jack James McGarry of the Vava Voom, which he created in 2008. "I first became interested in Tiki culture after a friend of mine made me a proper Trader Vic Mai Tai," he adds. "I thought the drink was fabulous, with a great depth and array of flavors. With the purchase of Grog Log and Sippin' Safari and a lot of Trader Vic's books, I began to get a real feel for what the Trader and Donn Beach were about and how they oper-

ated. I loved the way these two legends approached the making of drinks; they were never happy and were always trying to improve their work, and this is something that I felt I definitely shared with these guys." Jack's obsession with exotic cocktails eventually led him to his current gig at Sean Muldoon's Merchant Hotel bar (see Kon Tiki Ti-Punch above).

VELO

¾ ounce fresh lime juice
½ ounce passion fruit syrup
1 ounce St-Germain elderflower
    liqueur
1 ¼ ounces gin (Beefeater preferred)
4 dashes Peychaud's bitters

Shake well with ice cubes. Strain into a chilled cocktail coupe or wine glass.

"From 1994 to 2008 I toured with rock and jazz bands for a living, and this gave me the opportunity to travel all over the world," says musician and author James Teitelbaum, whose first priority in any new city was seeking out local Tiki bars. He rated his findings in the book Tiki Road Trip, which he's just followed up with Big Stone Head: Easter Island And Pop Culture. His Velo made it to the finals in a 2009 St-Germain cocktail contest; it started as a rum drink, but James soon found that "rum and St-Germain don't seem to play well together. Thinking of tropical drinks made with gin, like the Suffering Bastard and Polynesian Spell, I decided to try that combo instead. I needed something truly tropical and exotic in the mix to make it scream TIKI! Passion fruit was the answer, with some Peychaud's to cut the potentially overwhelming sweetness of passion fruit syrup combined with St-Germain. I also tried Angostura bitters, and orange bitters, but the Peychaud's seemed to work best."

VOYAGER

2 ounces light Puerto Rican or Virgin
    Islands rum
½ ounce fresh lime juice
½ ounce Bénédictine
½ ounce falernum
2 dashes Angostura bitters

Shake everything with ice cubes. Strain into an ice-filled old-fashioned glass. Garnish with a lime wedge.

As evidenced by the exotic drinks featured in his book The Essential Bartender's Guide and his webcast "The Cocktail Spirit," drink guru Robert Hess is no stranger to Tiki. "The craze of the 1940s and '50s centered around the notion of Polynesian restaurants being sort of a mini-vacation," says Robert, "so I chose to name this drink 'Voyager' to play on that notion. The fact that I'm a Star Trek fan played a small role as well."

XTABAY

½ ounce fresh lemon juice
½ ounce Domaine De Canton ginger liqueur
¾ ounce honey mix (see page 226)
2 ounces sumac-infused pisco*

Shake with ice cubes. Strain into a chilled cocktail glass.

*SUMAC-INFUSED PISCO: Add 2 ounces dried sumac to one 750ml bottle of Peruvian pisco (as opposed to Chilean pisco, which has different characteristics; Barsol is a good Peruvian brand). Let sit for five or six days, shaking the bottle occasionally. Strain through a coffee filter. Discard solids, then strain again through a fresh filter. When the liquid is rosy and clear, bottle it.

A paean to Peruvian soprano Yma Sumac's 1950 exotica album "Voice Of The Xtabay," this cocktail was created in 2008 by Martin Cate of Smuggler's Cove in San Francisco (see Dead Reckoning on page 197). Says he: "The Xtabay was born when I was reading about Middle Eastern food and the use of sumac, a dried berry that tastes lemony and very slightly salty. I thought that it would be great to infuse in spirits, and tried it in vodka, gin, rum, and pisco. Only the pisco was tasty, with the Peruvian grape must flavor working with the sumac really well. Once I had Peru and sumac in the same drink, Yma came immediately to mind, so it's named after her first album."

ZADARAN STORM

1 ounce fresh lime juice
½ ounce raspberry syrup*
½ ounce vanilla syrup
½ ounce maraschino liqueur
2 ounces dark Jamaican rum
Dash Angostura bitters
2 ounces ginger beer, chilled

Put everything — except ginger beer and vanilla bean — into a tall glass. Fill with crushed ice, add ginger beer, and stir for around 10 seconds to chill. Garnish with a vanilla bean, positioning the bean so you can get its aroma with every sip.

*RASPBERRY SYRUP: There are several brands on the market; we used Monin. You can also make your own: In a saucepan place 1 cup fresh or frozen raspberries, 1 cup sugar and 1 cup water. Simmer for 20 minutes, or until the berries are broken down and a bit syrupy. Strain to get the seeds out.

By Rick Stutz, 2008. Rick blogs on his Tiki-forward cocktail website kaiserpenguin. com. "Zadar, a bustling port in the 18th century, was the first to produce and export maraschino liqueur," he says. "The drink takes ginger beer and dark Jamaican rum from the Dark and Stormy — and so the name."

Don't worry about me...
I'm being taken care of!

(Below we list only the rums for which this book's recipes specifically call; if you're curious about other brands and types of rum, consult "The Bum On Rum" at www.beachbumberry.com.)

AMBER MARTINIQUE RUM The island of Martinique specializes in agricultural (*agricole*) rum made from fresh sugar cane, as opposed to *rhum industriel* distilled from sugar by-products like molasses. But agricole rum is not necessarily superior to industrial rum. We find many Martiniques unpleasantly earthy, with an agave-like nose and aftertaste that spoil mixed drinks. Even some expensive amber agricoles have this problem. Three that don't are Clément VSOP, J.M. Paille, and Neisson Élevé Sous Bois. (While we also recommend St. James Extra Old and Hors D'Age, as of this writing rumors are afoot that St. James will cease distribution in the U.S.)

APPLETON RUM See separate entries for Gold Jamaican rum and Dark Jamaican rum.

BARBADOS RUM There are white and gold Barbados rums, but this book's recipes only employ the latter (see separate entry for Gold Barbados rum).

COCKSPUR 12-YEAR V.S.O.R. RUM A tasty aged sipping rum, redolent of charred oak and honey. In mixed drinks, it's almost indistinguishable from Mount Gay Extra Old 12-year rum.

CRUZAN BLACK STRAP RUM While you can't substitute this black Virgin Islands rum for a dark Jamaican (Black Strap is just too molasses-intensive), in small doses it can really perk up a punch.

CRUZAN SINGLE BARREL ESTATE RUM A pleasant, relatively affordable aged sipping rum that also plays well in cocktails.

BARBANCOURT RUM A smooth, silky, Cognac-like export from Haiti. The eight-year-old Five Star is best for mixing.

COCONUT RUM The Bum generally has no use for flavored rums. Why buy orange rum when you can mix rum with orange juice? But coconut rum is actually useful, as it imparts coconut flavor to cocktails without your having to work around the thickness of coconut milk or the wateriness of coconut juice. Cruzan makes the smoothest, most natural-tasting coconut rum, but Bacardi Coco won't kill you. What *will* kill you are Malibu and Parrot Bay coconut rums; you're better off drinking suntan oil.

DARK JAMAICAN RUM Among the dark Jamaicans, Myers's tastes of molasses and Coruba of brown sugar, while Appleton Estate Extra conjures oak and caramel. When a recipe does not specifically call for one or the other, it's a matter of individual preference.

DEMERARA RUM The rich, aromatic, smoky "secret weapon" in most truly memorable tropical drinks, from Guyana. Two brands are spottily available in the US: Lemon Hart and El Dorado. Both companies make excellent 80-proof Demerara rums, but only Lemon Hart's 151-proof rum will work in the drinks that specifically call for it. (El Dorado's 151 lacks the heavy body and gunpowdery richness of Lemon Hart's.) Check the Lemon Hart label carefully — the 151-proof is differentiated from the 80-proof only by a tiny red triangle in the upper left corner.

FLOR DE CAÑA RUM A superior — and reasonably priced — product from Nicaragua. Flor De Caña's Extra Dry light rum, 4-year Gold rum, 5-year Black Label gold rum, and 7-year Grand Reserve gold rum all make excellent substitutes for their Puerto Rican and Cuban counterparts.

GOLD BARBADOS RUM Mellower and more fragrant than gold rums from elsewhere in the Caribbean. We like the personality of Cockspur Fine Rum and Doorly's 5-year, but the less assertive Mount Gay Eclipse also mixes well enough. English Harbour 5-year rum, from Antigua, subs nicely for gold Barbados rum.

GOLD JAMAICAN RUM Look for Appleton Special Gold. Appleton also makes an aged amber rum, Estate V/X, which works beautifully in recipes that call for gold Jamaican. (Caveat emptor: The Estate V/X bottle, label, and name are easily confused with its dark Jamaican sibling, Appleton Estate Extra.) If you live outside the U.S., ask around for Lemon Hart Gold Jamaica rum; it's great stuff, with more bite and less sweetness than the Appleton.

GOLD PUERTO RICAN RUM Bacardi 8 and Bacardi Añejo are both solid golds. Another brand, Ron Barrelito, also delivers. Even so, we generally substitute gold Virgin Islands rum for gold Puerto Rican, as the former is smoother and more aromatic. You can also safely substitute Flor De Caña gold rum from Nicaragua.

GOLD VIRGIN ISLANDS RUM Cruzan makes the best one, which up to 2009 they called "Estate Dark." Now they've switched the label to "Cruzan Aged Rum." We're not sure why. Did the estate go condo?

GOSLING'S BLACK SEAL RUM A dark rum from Bermuda. Personally we have no use for Gosling's, which to us tastes like root beer. But other tropaholics have figured out how to employ it in recipes we like, so we'll just shut our yap.

JAMAICAN RUM

See separate entries for Gold Jamaican rum and Dark Jamaican rum.

LIGHT (WHITE) PUERTO RICAN RUM This dry, clear spirit has long been the go-to rum for most tropicals, but today Puerto Rico no longer exports a decent light rum. Whenever you see a recipe calling for light Puerto Rican rum, we recommend substituting light Virgin Islands rum, which has a similar but rummier and smoother flavor profile. So does Flor De Caña Extra Dry from Nicaragua. From Barbados, Mount Gay Special Reserve is also a very good white rum, but it's overpriced (Mount Gay's cheaper white rum, Eclipse Silver, is rougher around the edges but still mixable). If you live outside the U.S., go for Cuba's Havana Club Silver — but study the label before buying, since Bacardi is slated to introduce its own Havana Club clone in the near future. White Martinique rums and white Jamaican rums (such as Appleton White or Myers's Platinum) should not be substituted for light Puerto Rican, as they're neither dry enough nor personable enough.

LIGHT (WHITE) VIRGIN ISLANDS RUM Cruzan dominates the market, and rightly so. Flor De Caña Extra Dry from Nicaragua is a good substitute. (See the Light Puerto Rican rum entry above for other alternatives.)

MARTINIQUE RUM Unaged white Martinique rum doesn't figure in any of this book's drinks, but you will need an aged amber if you want to make an authentic Mai Tai. (See separate entry for Amber Martinique rum.)

PUERTO RICAN RUM See separate entries for Light Puerto Rican Rum and Gold Puerto Rican rum.

SPICED RUM For years we've railed against the chemical taste of commercial spiced rum — which is made from the most rotgut base rum imaginable — but now even high-end designer cocktail bars are mixing with the insanely popular stuff. Much to our surprise, when we were tapped to do the same we found that spiced rum does have its uses in exotic drinks. Among current brands, Old New Orleans Cajun Spiced rum is best of show. It quickly goes downhill from there: Sailor Jerry's is rocket fuel, while Captain Morgan's Private Stock tastes like cinnamon schnapps with extra sugar. But Morgan's cheaper Original Spiced rum is actually quite mixable — go figure. Choose it over the well-reviewed but lackluster Foursquare spiced rum, which is made with a nice, mellow Barbados rum, but barely registers as being spiced.

VIRGIN ISLANDS RUM While comparable to Puerto Rican rums in body and character, Virgin Islands rums are generally more flavorful. See separate entries for Light Virgin Islands Rum and Gold Virgin Islands rum.

WRAY & NEPHEW OVERPROOF WHITE RUM The most popular rum in Jamaica. Jah only knows why. Still, handy for flaming drinks, and for the falernum recipe on page 197.

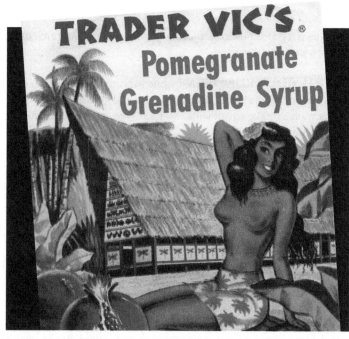

(For more detailed ingredient-related information, you can always ask the Bum at www.beachbumberry.com.)

ALMOND EXTRACT Available in your grocer's cooking section. Powerful stuff; dispense with an eye-dropper.

ANGOSTURA BITTERS Since the mid-1800s, the preferred flavoring agent of bars the world over. If your local liquor store doesn't carry it, your local supermarket does.

APRICOT BRANDY The Rolls Royce of apricot brandies is Rothman & Winter; the Volvo is Marie Brizard. The drinks in this book won't suffer if you want to economize with Bols, but beware of off-brands.

APRICOT NECTAR Nectars are basically fruit juice with added sugar. Looza makes a mixable apricot; if you can't find it, go with Kern's. Avoid Jumex and Goya.

AQUAVIT A Scandinavian liquor that derives its unique flavor from caraway seeds. Aalborg is a solid and affordable brand; Linie and O.P. Anderson are also good.

BÄRENJÄGER A German honey liqueur. Widely available.

BÉNÉDICTINE A French herbal liqueur with a whiff of lemon, made by Benedictine monks from a secret formula they've been distilling since 1510.

BLACKBERRY BRANDY Do not use a clear eau de vie in tropical drinks. You want the dark, liqueur-style blackberry-flavored brandy available from Bols, Hiram Walker, DeKuyper, and other brands.

BLUE CURACAO See Curacao.

BOURBON We like to mix with a hearty 90-proofer, such as Knob Creek or Buffalo Trace. You can also sub rye whiskey in tropical drinks that call for Bourbon (Sazerac rye is good stuff; Jim Beam rye is not.)

BRANDY If you have a trust fund, spring for a bottle of Gran Duque D'Alba. If you've been disinherited, plain old Christian Brothers or E&J will suffice for this book's recipes.

CAMPARI This bitter Italian aperitif is an acquired taste that we've never been able to acquire, so if you're new to Campari you should start with a small bottle (as of this writing they still sell 50ml minis).

CHAMBORD The brand name of the most widely distributed framboise (raspberry liqueur) on the U.S. market. Substitute at your peril; some off-brands are positively medicinal.

CHERRY HEERING A cherry liqueur from Denmark. You can sub a cheaper cherry-flavored brandy, but the result will fall somewhat flatter.

CINNAMON-INFUSED SUGAR SYRUP Beware of commercially available cinnamon syrups, which are too spicy to use in tropicals. The sole exception is Sonoma Syrup Company's, but it's expensive. Try making your own: Crush 3 cinnamon sticks and place in a saucepan with 1 cup sugar and 1 cup water. Bring to a boil, stirring until sugar is dissolved. Lower heat, cover saucepan, and simmer for 2 minutes. Remove saucepan from heat and, keeping it covered, let sit at least 2 hours before straining and bottling. It should keep about a month in the fridge.

COCONUT CREAM See Lopez Coconut Cream entry below.

COCONUT MILK A thick white substance obtained by shredding, soaking, and boiling coconut meat, then pressing it through a sieve. Or by going to a supermarket and buying it in cans. (Guess which option we choose to exercise.) Thai Kitchen Organic is a good brand, but any unsweetened variety will do.

COCONUT WATER The clear juice you get when you open a fresh coconut. Better grocers stock coconut water in convenient cans and cartons; make sure you buy a brand that's 100% pure coconut water, with no added sugar.

COFFEE-FLAVORED BRANDY Less sweet and more pugnacious than coffee liqueur (see below), for which it should not be substituted.

COFFEE LIQUEUR Kahlua and Tia Maria are the standard pours, but in most tropical drinks you can sub a cheaper off-brand and live to tell about it.

COFFEE SYRUP There are several on the market, but the only palatable brand we found was Fee Brothers Coffee Cordial syrup. Or make your own with the recipe on page 194.

COGNAC A brandy from the Cognac region of France. Don't spend a lot of money on a VSOP, since you'll be mixing it instead of sipping it. A VS will suffice; Martel and Hennessy make decent ones.

COINTREAU An orange liqueur that cannot be substituted with other orange liqueurs: Cointreau is drier than than triple sec, lighter than Grand Marnier, and more perfumey than Curacao. (One exception: Combier Liqueur d'Orange is not only comparable to Cointreau, but outperforms it with an intense orange bite and bouquet. It's a tad cheaper too.)

CREAM SHERRY A Spanish dessert wine, also called Sweet Sherry. The Harvey's Bristol Cream brand is ubiquitous.

CRÈME DE BANANA A banana liqueur, available from Bols, Marie Brizard, and many other brands. A good rule of thumb when considering those other brands: if the liqueur glows like yellow CT-scan dye, stop considering it.

CRÈME DE CACAO A chocolate-accented liqueur that comes in both brown and white (clear) varieties. There's no difference in taste; if a recipe specifies one over the other, it's for cosmetic reasons.

CRÈME DE CASSIS A liqueur made from black currant berries. Just about every liqueur company makes one; we notice very little difference between brands, so love the one you're with.

CURACAO A liqueur made from dried orange peels, bottled in both orange and blue colors. Marie Brizard and Señor Curacao are best, followed by Bols; if you live in Europe or Canada, look for the far superior Bols Dry Curacao, made with a rum base rather than a brandy base.

DEMERARA SUGAR SYRUP Equal parts brown demerara sugar (such as the Domino brand in your supermarket baking section) and water, heated until sugar dissolves (do not boil). Cool it and bottle it.

DOMAINE DE CANTON GINGER LIQUEUR A delicate, Cognac-based liqueur that lends itself nicely to exotic cocktails. Not cheap, but you're not likely to neglect your bottle.

EGG WHITE Worry no more about contracting salmonella from raw egg white — not when you can buy pasteurized 100% liquid egg whites, sold in cartons at your local supermarket. There are several nationally distributed brands; we use All Whites.

FALERNUM A ginger-lime syrup invented in the West Indies. Cocktailians have gone to war over which brand of falernum is the most authentic. Questions of provenance aside, we've found that Fee Brothers works best in vintage tropical drinks. (The epicurious can also make their own: see the recipe on page 197.)

FEE'S BITTERS While this book calls for Fee's Whiskey Barrel-Aged Bitters and Fee's Old Fashion bitters in only one recipe each, if you like creating your own cocktails you'll probably find yourself playing with both on a regular basis.

FRENCH VERMOUTH See Vermouth.

GALLIANO An herbal liqueur named after the Italian military hero. Popular in the 1970s as the main ingredient in a Harvey Wallbanger, but still widely available today.

GIN There are different types of gin, but the only type this book calls for is "London dry." Some solid brands: Martin Miller's, Beefeater, Tanqueray. While not technically a London dry, Plymouth gin also performs extremely well in tropicals.

GINGER BEER Not to be confused with ginger ale, which is milder and sweeter. Reed's Jamaican is our preferred brand (but check the label before buying, as Reed's also markets a ginger ale with almost identical packaging). Bundaberg also makes a very mixable ginger beer.

GINGER SYRUP Monin and Sonoma Syrup Company market this, but it's much cheaper to make your own: Cut a 2-inch long piece of fresh ginger into thin slices and place in a saucepan with 1 cup sugar and 1 cup water. Bring to a boil, stirring until sugar is dissolved. Lower heat, cover saucepan, and simmer for 2 minutes. Remove saucepan from heat and, keeping it covered, let sit for at least 2 hours before straining and bottling. Store it in the fridge.

GRAND MARNIER A Cognac-based orange liqueur. It pains us to say it, because this stuff is not cheap, but do not substitute with other orange liqueurs; Grand Marnier's flavor and body are sui generis.

GRAPEFRUIT JUICE You can get away with using commercial grapefruit juice, as long as it's 100% juice, unsweetened. We like the little 6-ounce cans, because we rarely use more than one at a time. Just make sure it's not "pink" or "ruby red" grapefruit juice, which is not only too sweet but will ruin the color of your drink. (Same goes if you're squeezing your own: only the yellowish fruit will work.)

GRENADINE This is supposed to be a pomegranate-flavored syrup, but most brands today have a horrible cherry taste. Fortunately, you can now buy actual pomegranate syrup: Amoretti, Monin, and Sonoma Syrup Company are all good. Whatever you do, stay away from Rose's so-called grenadine, which is little more than sugar water and red dye.

GUAVA NECTAR Kern's and Looza are loaded with sugar, but still better than the other brands we tried.

HERBSAINT An anise-flavored liqueur similar to Pernod (see entry below), but less expensive — and just as good.

HONEY MIX Equal parts clover honey and hot water from your tap or a kettle, stirred until honey dissolves. Cool it and bottle it. Store in the fridge, where it'll last several weeks.

ITALIAN VERMOUTH See Vermouth.

LEMON JUICE Squeeze your own. No exceptions. (See Lime Juice entry below.)

LICOR 43 A Spanish liqueur named after the 43 ingredients that go into it, chief among them vanilla. Also known as Cuarenta Y Tres.

LIME JUICE Always, always, *always* squeeze your own juice from fresh limes. Bottled lime juice is going to ruin your drink, no matter what the label promises. There is no way around this: If you're making drinks for 200 guests, you'll have to squeeze 200 limes. We don't like it any more than you do, but there it is.

LIMONCELLO A treacly Italian lemon liqueur, made by several companies. If you're just using it as a cocktail ingredient, don't bother spending a lot of money on a premium brand.

LOPEZ COCONUT CREAM Developed in 1954 as a labor-saving alternative to mixing sugar with coconut milk. Ignore other brands, such as Coco Real or Trader Vic's Ko Ko Kreme; Lopez was the first and is still the best. (If it congeals after opening, just agitate it with a spoon.)

LYCHEE NUT PURÉE To make it, shell, pit, and purée 1 pound of fresh lychee nuts in a blender; force the purée through a fine-mesh wire sieve and bottle it (this process should yield around 6 ounces). Otherwise, you'll have to order Funkin Lychee Purée online (it runs around $40 a kilo) or seek Perfect Purée Of Napa Valley's lychee puree ($25 for 27 ounces). Do not substitute lychees canned in syrup, or commercially available lychee juice (the latter is not only too thin, but the pear juice it's cut with throws off the flavor).

MACADAMIA NUT LIQUEUR Kahana Royale and Trader Vic's are good brands. (Come to think of it, they're the only brands.)

MANGO NECTAR Looza makes the best one; Kern's will do in a pinch.

MARASCHINO LIQUEUR Made in the Balkans from marasca cherries and their crushed pits. Not to be confused with maraschino cocktail cherries or syrup. Maraska, Stock, and Luxardo are all good brands.

NAVAN VANILLA LIQUEUR Two very good recipes in this book call for Navan, but because of its Cognac base the stuff is prohibitively expensive. Other vanilla liqueurs are too sweet and low-proof to substitute for Navan, but if you're skint you can try pinch-hitting with Licor 43 (just use a little less of it).

ORANGE BITTERS Unavailable for years, but now there are three good brands to choose from: Regan's, Fee Brothers, and Angostura (whose orange bitters, while excellent, are fruitier and less assertive than Regan's or Fee's).

ORANGE CURACAO See Curacao.

ORANGE FLOWER WATER A perfumey flavoring made from orange blossoms. Sold by Fee Brothers and several other companies; gourmet markets and better liquor stores carry it.

ORANGE JUICE Unlike lime and lemon juice, you can get away with using "not-from-concentrate" 100% juice in cartons — very helpful if you're making a bevy of drinks or a party punch.

ORGEAT SYRUP An almond-flavored sweetener. We like Premiere Essence, Trader Vic's, and Fee Brothers. If the artificial ingredients in all three brands offend you, try the recipe on page 207.

PARFAIT AMOUR A French cordial composed of citrus fruits, herbs, and brandy; dig that spacey lavender color. As of this writing, only Marie Brizard still manufactures it.

PAPAYA NECTAR Go with Kern's, for the simple reason that Looza doesn't make one.

PASSION FRUIT JUICE (A.K.A. LILIKOI, MARACUYÁ, OR GRANADILLA) There are few things more delectable than fresh-squeezed passion fruit juice — and few things more expensive to render. The last time we tried it, straining the flesh of eight ripe passion fruit yielded a paltry 3/4 ounce of juice, at a cost of $19 and change. Fortunately, you can squeak by with commercial passion fruit juice in your cocktails. Health food stores often carry the Ceres brand from South Africa, while Asian markets sometimes carry decent off-brand juices ("decent" meaning long on juice and short on added sugar and artificial ingredients).

PASSION FRUIT NECTAR Looza is the only palatable brand we found. Avoid Santa Cruz Organic, which tastes more like the grape and apple juices it's cut with.

PASSION FRUIT PURÉE If you live in an area with Latino markets or other specialty food stores, you're in luck: pick up a packet of frozen 100% passion fruit pulp under the La Fé (our favorite), Palmas, or Goya labels. The frozen pulp defrosts at room temperature in two hours, leaving you with a liquid purée that is cocktail-ready. Cost: very cheap, usually under $3 a packet. The other alternative is to pay through the nose by going online and ordering Funkin passion fruit purée (up to $40 per kilo, plus shipping). If you have the money, Funkin is a superb product that makes your exotic drinks sing. (But aside from the cost, the problem with Funkin is that after you open it, you've only got eight days to use it all before it spoils.)

PASSION FRUIT SYRUP These days it's hard to find a good one. Trader Vic's is now entirely artificial, and entirely awful. Monin is too orangey, Fee Bothers Golden too peach-flavored, and Torani ... don't ask. Finest Call offers a "Passion Fruit Purée Mix" that is, in effect, a passion fruit syrup — and very mixable, although some readers have judged it a little too thin. But instead of buying a commercial passion fruit syrup, you're much better off making your own. There's a cheap way to do this, and an expensive way. Expensive will taste better (surprise!), but not by all that much. Here's the cheap way: Pick up a packet of frozen 100% passion fruit pulp (see Passion Fruit Purée entry above for brand and availability info). Mix the defrosted pulp in equal parts with sugar syrup (see entry below) and you're done. It will last two or three days in the fridge. And here's the expensive way: order Funkin passion fruit purée online (see Passion Fruit Purée entry above for info). It makes a delicious syrup when mixed in equal parts with sugar syrup. (Whatever path you take, do not try to make a syrup with commercial passion fruit juices or nectars, such as Ceres and Looza, which are already cut with sugar, water, and other ingredients that render them unsuitable as a syrup base.)

PEACH BRANDY Look for Marie Brizard or Bols. Admit defeat and go with DeKuyper or Hiram Walker only if that's all your local grog shops offer.

PERNOD An anise-flavored liqueur that Don The Beachcomber used in very small doses to dimensionalize drinks with a dark rum base. (See Herbsaint entry for a cheaper alternative.)

PEYCHAUD'S BITTERS A 200-year-old formula invented by New Orleans druggist Antoine Peychaud; sweeter and fruitier than

Angostura (for which Peychaud's is not a substitute).

PIMENTO LIQUEUR Not made from the kind of pimentos you stuff into olives, but from the pimento berry — otherwise known as allspice. In 1998 you could still find bottles of the luscious Wray & Nephew liqueur, but those disappeared from shelves almost as soon as the *Grog Log* went to print. After a ten-year drought, pimento is finally available again — in the form of St. Elizabeth Allspice Dram. To avoid confusion, importer Haus Alpenz wisely decided not to call this new product pimento liqueur, but that's what it is — and it works beautifully in this book's recipes. A blander and sweeter brand, Berry Hill, is also available online from Jamaica, but as long as the far superior St. Elizabeth is on the market there's no point in ordering Berry Hill. (For a cheaper alternative to both, make your own pimento liqueur with the recipe on page 208.)

PINEAPPLE JUICE To minimize wastage, we use the 6-ounce cans of Dole's 100% pineapple juice. Any other brand you buy should be unsweetened.

PISCO A clear brandy distilled from South American grapes, pisco is the national drink of both Peru and Chile. There are lots of brands to choose from; we buy Capel because it comes in a bottle shaped like an Easter Island moai. Inca Pisco can also be found in cool pre-Columbian decanters, ranging from Olmec to Incan idols. (If you haven't guessed from our purchasing criteria, we don't take Pisco all that seriously as a premium spirit — but the recipes in this book that call for it definitely justify having a bottle around.)

POMEGRANATE SYRUP See Grenadine.

PORT A dessert wine from Portugal. Tawny Ports are nuttier, drier, and generally preferable to Ruby Ports, but both will work in this book's recipes. Once decanted, Port goes bad after a few weeks, so don't spend a lot of money unless you plan on killing the bottle fairly soon (very easy to do if you chase it with a platter of cheese and sliced apple).

ROSE'S LIME JUICE CORDIAL Rose's is not a substitute for fresh-squeezed lime juice, but a lime-flavored sweetener. Use only when a recipe calls for it by name.

SLOE GIN A liqueur made from sloe berries and gin (although cheaper brands use neutral spirits). Plymouth makes the best one.

ST-GERMAIN ELDERFLOWER LIQUEUR St-Germain claims that its flowers are hand-picked and wheeled to the distillery by little old Alpine villagers on bicycles. If you buy that, we have a bridge we'd like to sell you (it connects Hawaii to the mainland). But St-Germain has become the darling of the drinkie set for a reason; its novel flavor works well in cocktails.

SUGAR SYRUP Also known as simple syrup or rock candy syrup. There are many brands to choose from; opt for one made with pure cane sugar rather than the justly maligned high fructose corn syrup. Or make it yourself: Place 1 cup sugar and 1 cup water in a saucepan. Heat but do not boil, stirring until sugar is thoroughly dissolved. Then bottle the syrup and set aside to cool.

TAWNY PORT See Port.

TEQUILA The cheap stuff can get pretty nasty; don't settle for less than a 100% agave bottling, preferably an aged reposado.

TRIPLE SEC In this book's recipes, any medium-priced brand of triple sec will do. (Do not substitute another type of orange liqueur, such as Cointreau or Grand Marnier, which have different flavor profiles.)

VANILLA EXTRACT Look for it in the baking section of your local grocery store. Apply one drop at a time, or it will turn your drink into liquid Nilla Wafers.

VANILLA SYRUP There are many serviceable brands on the market, but Fee Brothers French Vanilla Cordial syrup is the richest.

VERMOUTH An aperitif wine infused with botanicals. Italian (red) vermouth is on the sweet side; Carpano Antica is excellent, but hard to find and expensive when you do — while Martini & Rossi Rosso is affordable and everywhere. French (white) vermouth is dry and straw-colored; look for Noilly Prat Dry or Cinzano Extra Dry. Once you open it, keep vermouth in the fridge and replace it after three months, ere it goes bad.

VODKA A neutral spirit, which simply means that it has no flavor of its own. People tell us that some vodkas "taste" better than others, but as far as we're concerned, any name brand will do.

The Total Recipe Index alphabetically lists every drink in this book. For new and newly discovered vintage recipes unique to this edition, go directly to the Previously Unpublished Recipes Index on page 234. To locate a recipe by its base liquor or other specific category (such as dessert drinks, hot drinks, party punches, etc.), consult the Recipes By Category Index starting on page 235.

RECIPES BY CATEGORY

DESSERT DRINKS

COGNAC DRINKS

GIN DRINKS

HOT DRINKS

ISLAND OF MISFIT DRINKS (MIXED BASE LIQUORS)

NONALCOHOLIC DRINKS

OKOLEHAU DRINKS

PARTY PUNCHES

ORIGINAL PHOTOGRAPHY CREDITS

Jonpaul Balak: 49, 52, 81, 100, 126 (bottom), 144, 154 (both photos), 161, 177. Jamie Boudreau: 215. Rikki Brodrick: 205. Greg Burman: 211. Martin Cate: 196. Martin Doudoroff: 40, 89, 97, 140. Bosko Hrnjak: 11, 173, 248. Annene Kaye: 47, 51, 66, 68, 78 (bottom), 101, 102 (top), 113, 121, 130 (bottom), 142 (top), 146, 155, 158, 169, 170, 179, 183, 187, 218. Sven Kirsten: 17, 105 (bottom). Kevin Kidney: 131, 141. Scott Lindgren: 91 (bottom), 103. Cass McClure: 31, 33, 41, 42, 53, 56, 58, 73 (drink), 78 (top), 79, 87, 95, 96, 115, 117, 153, 157, 165, 168, 188, 191. Brian Powers: 199.

ABOUT THE BUM

Jeff "Beachbum" Berry is the author of four previous books on vintage Tiki drinks and cuisine, which *Los Angeles* magazine called "the keys to the tropical kingdom."

He's been profiled in the *New York Times*, *Imbibe* magazine, Salon.com, the *New Orleans Times-Picayune*, Saveur.com, and the *Tampa Tribune*; he's also been featured in the *Washington Post* and *The Wall Street Journal*, and has appeared on Martha Stewart Living Radio and Radio Margaritaville.

His original cocktail recipes have been printed in publications around the world, most recently the 67th edition of the *Mr. Boston Official Bartenders Guide*. In 2008 he created the cocktail menu for the Luau in Beverly Hills, which the *New York Times* cited as one of the nation's 24 "Bars on The Cutting Edge." With Martin Doudoroff, he co-created "Tiki+" for iPhone and iPod Touch, a drink recipe app which *Macworld* magazine called "beautifully rendered and, thanks to Berry's tireless reporting, impeccably sourced."

The Beachbum currently conducts tropical drink seminars and tastings across the U.S. and Europe. He serves on the advisory board of the Museum Of The American Cocktail.

Although the Bum has no fixed address, you can always contact him at www.beachbumberry.com.

CPSIA information can be obtained at www.ICGtesting.com
Printed in the USA
BVOW10s0840291214

381192BV00002B/2/P